I0820211

"*Seeds of Racial Healing* is one of those books you don't just read—you feel it. Sheila Wise Rowe doesn't just write about healing; she walks with you through it. Each devotion is honest, reflective, and grounded in lived experience and deep faith. As someone who has lived through racialized trauma and grief and navigated the long road to healing, I felt both seen and encouraged in these pages. This book offers space to breathe, be honest with God, and believe healing is still possible. Sheila Wise Rowe has given us a gift—a steady companion for the journey when the weight feels too heavy."

Terence Lester, founder of Love Beyond Walls and author of *I See You* and *From Dropout to Doctorate*

"Sheila Wise Rowe is the sage for our souls. With tender grace and abundant care, she guides us into the arms of the Savior to experience the healing power of God. The sin of racism wounds us all. This book is a salve that mends our brokenness and positions us to thrive together in Christ!"

Nicole Massie Martin, author of *Nailing It* and CT president and CEO

"I found myself, like Hagar, saying, 'You are the God who sees *me*!' Sheila Wise Rowe has masterfully narrated a devotional in a way that speaks to the very real lived experiences of a group of people who for generations have been oppressed and traumatized. Sheila has thoughtfully and artistically addressed the cultural nuances that are so often overlooked for those who seek healing in God's Word. *Well done*!"

Monique Gadson, associate professor of counseling psychology at The Seattle School of Theology and Psychology

"Sheila Wise Rowe is a safe voice, offering a holy nudge to remember God as our hope and care amid loss and racial trauma. *Seeds of Racial Healing* is a timely encouragement, a deep exhale, and a source of comfort for weary sojourners, reminding us that even amid the pressures and unrest of our world, it is God who plants seeds of hope, healing, and restoration in our hearts."

Natasha Smith, author of *Can You Just Sit with Me?* and *Black Woman Grief*

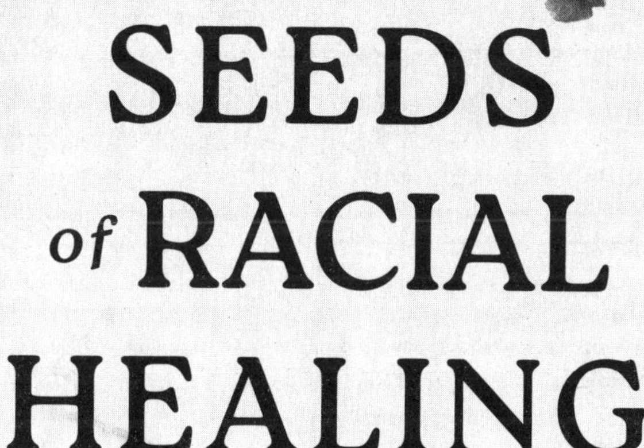

SEEDS *of* RACIAL HEALING

52 DEVOTIONS FOR NAVIGATING THROUGH TRAUMA

Sheila Wise Rowe

An imprint of InterVarsity Press
Downers Grove, Illinois

InterVarsity Press
P.O. Box 1400 | Downers Grove, IL 60515-1426
ivpress.com | email@ivpress.com

InterVarsity Press® is the publishing division of InterVarsity Christian Fellowship/USA®.
For more information, visit intervarsity.org.

Published in association with Books & Such Literary Management, 52 Mission Circle, Suite 122, PMB 170, Santa Rosa, CA 95409-5370, www.booksandsuch.com.

Cover design: Faceout Studio
Interior design: Jeanna Wiggins
Image: © Simon McGill / Moment via Getty Images

ISBN 978-1-5140-0617-7 (print) | ISBN 978-1-5140-0618-4 (digital)

Printed in Colombia ♾

Library of Congress Cataloging-in-Publication Data
A catalog record for this book is available from the Library of Congress.

31 30 29 28 27 26 | 8 7 6 5 4 3 2 1

DEDICATED TO

The Lord,

in whose presence I find

peace and joy.

Mae Wise,

my heart's first earthly home.

My dear Nicholas,

forever loving, encouraging,

and welcoming me.

CONTENTS

PART 4: BECOMING GROWN, DAYS 33-42

PART 5: SOW, TEND, AND HARVEST, DAYS 43-52

INTRODUCTION

You have been given a new birth. It was from a seed that cannot die. This new life is from the Word of God which lives forever.

1 Peter 1:23 (NLV)

We are born from a seed that cannot die. 1 Peter 1:23 speaks the truth about who we really are.

Although systemic racism, racial trauma, and relational dysfunction deny it, Black, Indigenous, Latino/a, Asian, Pacific Islanders, and other folk of color (BIPOC) are created in the image of God. Furthermore, we are not a monolith. We come from particular cultures and ethnicities and have similarities and differences in how we experience life and community. This devotional invites us to consider our race and culture as we encounter various seed metaphors that highlight things we have in common. Some explicitly refer to seeds of racial healing and blessing sown by God, while others are seeds of lies, distortions, and trauma sown into our lives and communities.

One thing BIPOC have in common is how metaphorically noxious seeds continue to be sown into our lives, families, and communities as they have for generations. These seeds produce weeds that spring up and try to choke out new growth of hope, joy, healing, and perseverance. Racism takes a toll on us. We cry out in prayer and protest bias, racist assaults, immigration crackdowns, the erasure of our history, and miscarriages of justice. Some moments may also tap into memories of past and current struggles. In 2 Corinthians 4:8-9 (NIV), we read how "we are hard pressed on every side, but not crushed; perplexed, but not in despair; persecuted, but not abandoned; struck down, but not destroyed." However, at any given moment we may feel like we're being crushed and abandoned.

This is how I felt after signing the contract to write this devotional. Its focus was to help BIPOC folk walk through daily life more aware of God—embracing life and pursuing healing and justice—while still confronting interpersonal racism, bias, and systemic oppression. I was to submit it to my publisher later in the year. Then in June of that year, my dear mother, called Momae, passed away. While her health had steadily declined over many years, I wasn't fully in touch with how I walked through each day carrying anticipatory grief. I knew that losing mom would happen, but then again, I didn't. Along the way I felt profound exhaustion, waves of sadness, and yet inexplicable joy.

Similarly, so much of racial healing for BIPOC is about addressing racial trauma, anticipatory and other forms of grief and injustice, while experiencing pockets of joy and celebration. I've been on a three-year journey to complete this devotional. It contains seeds of racial healing that are not only for you but also for me. I am processing my own grief and racial trauma while struggling to stay the course as I feel the pull to be more, do more, say more, and always be "on." The same may be true for you. Additionally, we may be expected to educate everyone about race or tend to other folks' pain, grief, and terror—all the while carrying our own. Then occasionally, we're able to rejoice over small and large victories such as personal, emotional, or communal breakthroughs or convictions. We hunger for justice, persevere, but remain deeply in need of rest.

We are not alone in the fight. Psalm 69:32-33 (NRSV) tells us,

> Let the oppressed see it and be glad;
> you who seek God, let your hearts revive.
> For the Lord hears the needy,
> and does not despise his own who are in bonds.

Our God is ever present, and the Scriptures also emphasize the importance of other folk. Many of us know the importance of communal care over rugged individualism. Although you may choose to go through the *Seeds of Racial Healing* devotional solo, I suggest inviting a trusted friend or small group to join you. We need safe-enough, trustworthy, and indispensable sisters and brothers in Christ called by God to pray, love, walk, and work alongside us with a tool in one hand and a spiritual weapon in the other.

In this devotional I hope you will find encouragement and moments to pause, heal, hope, reset, revive, and respond. Like every plant that starts as a seed deep in the earth, hidden from public view, growth is literally and figuratively underground. Moreover, after the seed sprouts, it will go through cycles for the rest of its life. Each year, it will endure a period when it must stop working, shut down its processes, shed its outer coat, turn inward, rest, and preserve itself. Sometimes that period is relatively gentle, but often it is difficult, with intense cold and storms that test its ability to persevere. If the seed endures, it develops perseverance. Then it returns to work in the spring, preparing to sprout, then bloom.

As you deeply engage these fifty-two devotions, may you begin to heal, dream again, and perhaps for the first time hear God's plan for your life and the lives of those in your community. It can be immensely helpful and healing to keep a journal to record your journey.

The *Seeds of Racial Healing* devotional consists of five themes that highlight issues addressed on this journey: the sower and the seeds; the soil of your story; the weeds among the wheat; becoming grown; and sow, tend, and harvest. Each theme has ten to twelve devotions that address the theme and incorporate Bible verses and personal or scriptural stories that encourage and challenge. Each devotion concludes with a personal or communal question to contemplate and a listening or breath prayer. There may also be a word of encouragement gleaned from the Scriptures or heard while I engaged in listening prayer. Finally, there may be specific creative practices or action steps to take. My prayer is that with each devotion, we embrace more of the truth that we are beloved BIPOC, children of God, born again from an imperishable seed.

PART 1

The Sower and the Seeds

Days 1-10

Listen! A farmer went out to plant some seeds. As he scattered them across his field, some seeds fell on a footpath, and the birds came and ate them. Other seeds fell on shallow soil with underlying rock. The seeds sprouted quickly because the soil was shallow. But the plants soon wilted under the hot sun, and since they didn't have deep roots, they died. Other seeds fell among thorns that grew up and choked out the tender plants. Still other seeds fell on fertile soil, and they produced a crop that was thirty, sixty, and even a hundred times as much as had been planted! Anyone with ears to hear should listen and understand.

MATTHEW 13:3-9

DAY 1

IMPERISHABLE SEED

Those who plant in tears
will harvest with shouts of joy.
They weep as they go to plant their seed,
but they sing as they return with the harvest.

PSALM 126:5-6

As a child, I was clueless about how our Nana and Grandaddy held tightly onto their farm on the Eastern Shore of Virginia. They faced obstacles, including systemic racism, that prevented them from getting a fair market price for their crops. They were at the mercy of the fickleness of harsh weather that quickly destroys a fragile seedling or the entire crop. Each year in the heat of summer, my family descended upon our grandparents' farm. Every day after breakfast, my siblings and I raced down dusty roads. Out of breath, thirsty, and hungry at the strawberry patch, we grabbed as much as we could eat. It was a mystery which strawberry seeds planted in the ground endured to become what they were meant to be. We simply enjoyed the sweetness of the fruit when the crop was good or were disappointed when it wasn't.

In the parable of the sower, Jesus makes an excellent metaphor for some of the above- and below-ground challenges that seeds face. While the parable of the sower is about the kingdom of God, notice it doesn't focus on the condition of the seed. Just like the seed in the parable, we are influenced by the soil or environment we are planted in. We may live, work, and worship in environments that we assumed were safe enough only to discover they were not. We've had experiences that caused pain and racial trauma. Our stories may include facing opposition over which we lashed out, remained silent, or were silenced.

There's a saying in activist circles: "They tried to bury us. They didn't know we were seeds." Meditate on 1 Peter 1:23 (NLV): "You have been given a new birth. It was from a seed that cannot die. This new life is from the Word of God which lives forever." This is an essential verse that helps us embark on this healing journey. This verse calls us to remember who and whose we are. We are born of imperishable seed. This is the truth of who we really are, and our lives matter to God. We see how a plant's seeds are dispersed via the wind, water, animals, people, explosion, and fire. These seeds then land on ground and may grow into new plants. However, unlike these average seeds that are subject to the environment, elements, and nature, we cannot be destroyed. Although the enemy of our souls would cause us to doubt this truth, we may be pressed down, persecuted, and struck down, but we are not destroyed. Although we face ongoing frustrations and assaults that try to sway our attention from what the Lord has called us to, all is not lost. In the Scriptures we read stories of the power, sovereignty, and faithfulness of God, through whom we have been born again, not of perishable seed, but of imperishable. On this journey called life, the Lord is our refuge and strength, an ever-present help in trouble. So we lament—"a way of seeing, standing, and wrestling or arguing with God, and thus a way of hoping in the midst of ruins." Prayers of lament help to keep our eyes on the Lord who hears our every cry. Then we may see how God is woven throughout the stories of our lives. Amid past and current experiences of racism, we can look for the

Lord who fights for us and brings light and love even in the smallest ways.

A WORD OF ENCOURAGEMENT In prayer I heard, "Trust me, I have a greater agenda of healing your trauma and restoring your peace with the gift of my peace. Take quiet moments to rest and reflect with me. I will speak to you during those times to bring clarity and vision for the now and new seasons of your life."

REFLECT Are you having difficulty trusting and believing that healing, justice, or both are possible for us? If so, when you are ready, honestly tell the Lord how you feel, lament, and ask for help to take the next step.

PRAYER

> But you, Sovereign Lord,
> help me for your name's sake;
> out of the goodness of your love, deliver me.
> For I am poor and needy,
> and my heart is wounded within me.
> (Psalm 109:21-22 NIV)

Show me where the soil in my life is hard, rocky, thorny, or fertile. As I lament, help me trust you to sow seeds that revive me as I heal from racial trauma. In Jesus' name, amen.

DAY 2

THE SOWER

He [or she] who watches the wind will not plant his seeds.
And he [or she] who looks at the clouds will not gather the food.
Just as you do not know the path of the wind or how
the bones are made of a child yet to be born, so you
do not know the work of God Who makes all things.

ECCLESIASTES 11:4-5 (NLV)

Just as the earth has its cycle and seasons, so do we. In the Northeast of the United States, the air is frigid cold, Paris is gloomy and gray, while in Johannesburg, South Africa, the sun shines bright. No matter where you are on this planet, at a moment's notice the temperature can change, or there's a torrential downpour, a tornado, or a balmy breeze. Such is it with us. The world cries out for justice, balance, and order, and we also attempt to find our own equilibrium. But apart from God, this is momentary or futile, although we try our hardest. Although we were fearfully and wonderfully made, knit together in our mother's wombs (see Psalm 139:13-14), we are also children of God desperately in need of rest.

So many of us are processing racial trauma and grief in life and in our engagement in justice work. We've all felt the frustration of sowing what we thought was promising seed. We hoped for transformation only to find we moved two steps forward then one step back. We've seen incremental change but also backlash. Many of us have labored long and hard, but the pain of past and present racism is real. It has affected our nervous systems, hormones, minds, and bodies. We can't fully relax, then another racist incident creates this endless racial trauma loop. We bear unhealed wounds, traumatic racial histories, and still we must deal with microaggressions and almost daily assaults on our dignity and character. The enormity of the pain and terror in and around us feels like a gray cloud hovering above. Are we reluctant to sow the seeds that God has given us because we are fixated on the clouds? Honestly, it's challenging to continue to sow with little to no guarantee of success. Ecclesiastes 11:4-5 reminds us God controls whether the seed will germinate or how it will keep growing. As we read in Matthew 13:3-9, it may seem that God haphazardly scatters seed and doesn't seem concerned about how, when, and where it's sown. But our God is the Creator, the Sower of good seed, and the Giver of life.

I remember the night in 2000 when we watched a TV special about how HIV/AIDS was devastating South Africa. I cried throughout the show. In 2001 we joined a racially diverse mission team to Johannesburg, South Africa, to serve those impacted by HIV/AIDS. After a week of ministry, we celebrated at a game reserve. In this stunning beauty, we saw racism rear its ugly head as the Black waiters faced humiliation from the White lodge guests. There was also racial conflict within our mission team. I felt a profound sense of the brutality and racial trauma that Black South Africans had and were still facing. I felt a sense of Jesus' heart for South Africa and her people. Just as Jesus wept over Jerusalem, I (uncharacteristically) publicly wept for the men at the lodge and for Black South Africans. Then I had to confront the racism on our team. I came away questioning if I could ever really trust White people. I wept for myself, our team, and Black folk back home. I cried for hours. The next day, we left Johannesburg. I was depleted but felt a prompting in my heart: *One day you will return*. Although seeds were planted that week, it took five years before we moved.

At some point we all may find the sower has unexpectantly planted us where we can experience deeper trust. God helps us to thrive while we wait or actively pursue change wherever we are planted. As our seeds are sown, we can entrust the results to the Lord. And along the way, the Holy Spirit gives insight. We begin to unearth truths about racism and racial trauma: how they affect us, where the roots are, and what our current triggers are. Increasingly we experience an undergirding of peace and reminders that God, the Sower, is continually at work delivering us, healing us, and encouraging new life to take root.

A WORD OF ENCOURAGEMENT In prayer I heard, "I give you the waters of refreshment for the dry and weary places in your heart and mind. Even triggers and trauma will not stop you from persevering in love and celebrating life more fully."

REFLECT How can you face your triggers with Jesus? Are there people who will listen to your whole story?

BREATH PRAYER Silently or aloud, speak this truth: The Lord is—merciful and compassionate. Then to a count of four while inhaling, silently repeat the words "The Lord is." Hold your breath to a count of four, and then slowly exhale to a count of four, silently repeating the words "merciful and compassionate."

DAY 3

ROOTED IN GOD

Then Christ will make his home in your hearts as you trust in him. Your roots will grow down into God's love and keep you strong.

Ephesians 3:17

There were moments early in our faith walks when we saw Abba so clearly tending to our wounds and addressing injustice. We felt the closeness of God's love. Do you remember those days of delight and wonder? God extended a lifeline, you grabbed hold, and your faith ran deep. Then life happened—the wounds and the wonder of it all. Like a child, we may wail, feeling abandoned, lacking the sense of closeness we once had. We may question whether God is still here or ever was.

Then like the perfect parent, God, our Creator, says he never left.

Throughout all eternity God has existed as Father, Son, and Holy Spirit, interacting with one another in love. God offers this profound love to each of us. In Genesis 1:27 we read how we are created in the *imago Dei*—the image of our triune God. God looked over all he had made, and he saw that it was very good! The first human family was created and "the man and his wife were both naked, but they felt no shame" (Genesis 2:25). The family walked with God in the Garden and knew him as the source of love, rest, peace, and completeness. Adam and Eve had no fear of harm or abuse; they were at home. After they sinned, they lost their home in the Garden but not God's love.

Since then, we all ache for what was lost—so much so that we try to find, create, or maintain something we hope meets our longing to be rooted in God again. But God so loved the world and poured out his compassion that he gave his Son, Jesus, to save our souls. Sometimes, however, we don't recognize the hand of God moving through folk around us. When they extend compassion, care, time, and attention, it can be God wooing us through them. Sometimes we may mistakenly blame the Lord for the mayhem and trauma we've suffered, for our inability to relate well to God and each other. Thanks be to God, he is always working to restore our relationships with himself and each other. Jesus saved us and promised that we are not left alone as orphans hoping someone will love us. Jesus loves us and cleanses and heals our wounds. Hebrews 4:15 (NRSV) tells us how he gets us: "For we do not have a high priest who is unable to sympathize with our weaknesses, but we have one who in every respect has been tested as we are, yet without sin." Jesus knows feelings of powerlessness and abandonment, yet he gave up his life as the ultimate sacrifice for our sin and what was done against us. His resurrection signifies his power to absorb our suffering and to release its power over us. Yet Jesus offers much more. In John 10:10, Jesus tells us although "the thief's purpose is to steal and kill and destroy. My purpose is to give them a rich and satisfying life."

On this healing journey, it's also essential to remember this and to listen for the voice of the Holy Spirit that can be small, almost imperceptible. This voice also may be loud and clear and open doors in surprising ways when we least expect it. Perhaps we may be prompted to reach out in love to those around us to simply be a present and a presence. The Spirit whispers that we are beloved, made of imperishable seed and an imperishable love rooted in our triune God. When our lives are planted in God, our roots are deep and our faith grows strong.

REFLECT Do you struggle to stay rooted in God and believe Jesus' promise of a more satisfying life?

PRACTICE As you wrap your arms around yourself, ask the Holy Spirit to bring you into the truth of the Lord's great compassion and care for you.

BREATH PRAYER Breathe in a count of four, hold a count of four, and exhale a count of four: "I am beloved and belong (hold)—(exhale) I am rooted in God."

DAY 4 

SEEDBED

And the seeds that fell on the good soil represent honest,
good-hearted people who hear God's word,
cling to it, and patiently produce a huge harvest.

Luke 8:15

A seedbed may be an environment or experience where different seeds are planted all at once. Some are good seeds that affirm faith, love, hopes, or dreams. For many of us, there may also be seeds of fear, anxiety, or unbelief that tell us that the Lord will not take care of us. We may struggle to see God's hand at work in our lives or to trust his heart. So we believe we must take care of ourselves.

Remember the shock of the death of Jesus Christ on the cross. The day after his crucifixion and burial was a day of tension and holding in place. Some won't dwell on that day in between, as we are on the way to celebrate the resurrection on Sunday. Saturday can feel a bit anticlimactic. But imagine you didn't know how the story would turn out. The disciples and followers thought that this time around, things would be different. They watched in awe as Jesus stood up to the Pharisees, performed miracles, healed folk, and even raised the dead. Now his followers saw everything fall to pieces: the promise of a new Israel, the Roman yoke thrown off, the new kingdom where they would rule with Christ as opposed to remaining marginalized. And most hurtful of all, Jesus, the Messiah, the new king, hung on a cross, the symbol of criminality and shame, like a nobody. For his followers, his brutish death meant they might be next, so they hid themselves as best they could. The disorientation was deep. The big "now what?" hung in the air.

We also may feel like this. As a BIPOC, we may be experiencing disappointment and despair over an impossible situation in which we feel trapped and locked up in fear. Seeds of fear and unbelief may make us feel like fools for having trusted again. If you feel this way, or have ever felt this way, then it is Saturday. We may wait while evidence of loss is all around. We may have a crisis of faith, of hope, of confusion—or feel an overwhelming need for clarity. The disciples confronted the same things that we battle. We see before, during, and after the cross; they had trouble understanding Jesus and what his mission was all about. Each of them came into the season with their own set of agendas. Peter thought this was all about a rebellion. Judas basically gave up and decided he might as well make some money out of it. Jesus' mother, Mary, and the women mourned while holding onto hope. As we look at these ones, we see glimpses of our own struggles during seasons where our seedbeds seem filled with seeds of doubt and struggles to understand and persevere. In the garden of Gethsemane, Jesus asked the disciples to watch and pray, but they kept falling asleep. They were experiencing disenfranchised grief that couldn't be openly acknowledged and anticipatory grief over the impending loss. This weighed heavily on them.

We know how the story with Jesus Christ turned out—we have heard it a million times—but the death of Jesus is not a one-off thing. Yes, it happened once, but the hearts and minds of men and women the world over relive the death of dreams and hopes time and time again, and every time we do, Jesus—the One who is risen—comes again. He reminds us that even though we do not know how our stories will turn out, he does know. Jesus understands the Saturday we may be in. Again, he says, his resurrection and victory over death is constantly at hand. Because Jesus rose from the dead, resurrection is always present with him; he is the resurrection. He loves us and calls us to believe. Loss, grief, and death don't have the final word. Jesus does. Jesus takes our hopes and plants them in his seedbed alongside the seeds of others who are "honest, good-hearted folk who hear God's word, cling to it, and patiently produce a huge harvest" (Luke 8:15).

A WORD OF ENCOURAGEMENT In prayer I heard, "I am the living Word. You can place all your disappointments, racial trauma, hopes that look dead, and your pain at the foot of the cross. Wait and walk with me as I redeem each part of your story."

REFLECT What do you need to surrender as you wait on Saturday?

PRACTICE Write your hopes and dreams in a poem or haiku. (A haiku is a three-line poem with five syllables on the first line, seven syllables on the second, and five syllables on the third line.)

BREATH PRAYER Place your hand on your heart, breathe, and pray: "Here's my heart Lord (hold)—(exhale) speak what is true."

DAY 5

SEEDS OF WELCOME

Just as our bodies have many parts and each part has a special function, so it is with Christ's body. We are many parts of one body, and we all belong to each other.

ROMANS 12:4-5

Sometimes God uses nature to make a point. In our yard in Johannesburg, a well-fed, bright yellow Southern Masked Weaver built an elaborate nest on a branch. He did not strive to create the raw material. He simply looked for what was usable, sustainable, and he ignored the rest. He gathered fresh blades of grass, seed, stems, and leaves from nearby trees, all provided by our Creator. This Weaver diligently constructed a home, unsure whether it would stand strong against the wind and predators. Most important, he built hoping it would be acceptable to his future mate. If it wasn't good enough, he'd deconstruct the nest and rebuild again and again until he got it right. I watched him do this until finally he welcomed his mate home.

Welcome. This simple word speaks to a core issue many of us struggle with. As I watched the birds, I thought of how we all long for a home or a place of welcome. But many of us feel unwelcomed. Being loved, cared for, and noticed by others feels conditional based on what we say or do. I once thought Abba Father was like many of the men I encountered as I grew up: undependable or haphazard in extending welcome to women. This created a disrupted attachment between God and me, and mostly with men, but also with women. Relational dysfunction like this trains us to fear. So we tune into the smallest glimpses of unwelcome in the faces of others. We search for welcome.

But there is One who understands everything we face, and he persevered through it: Jesus. He prayed to the Father to give us the Holy Spirit to walk with us. In the book of Genesis, God declared everything was very good, except for one thing: being alone (i.e., not belonging or being welcomed). God has ordained our healing to be worked out in the context of relationships. We need other believers to remind us of who we really are and that we are welcomed. As they persevere with and pray for us, we begin to experience God releasing his bread and life-giving water through them. Slowly we are learning how to be securely attached to God and others. Our relationships grow deeper, we feel seen, met, accepted, and at times challenged. This is all good. However, in the future we will face people and institutions that deem us unacceptable. In these places we may never find the needed material to create a home. So, like the weaver bird, we may stay and build again, or like Jesus instructed his disciples, shake the dust off our feet.

A WORD OF ENCOURAGEMENT In prayer I heard, "May you find within the context of the community that I have given you a safe place of people committed to you—where your healing can take place, where you can be free to be yourself. I don't call you to suffer in isolation. I send folks to you as a gift so that you may walk in greater wholeness and holiness. Watch for them."

REFLECT Is social media helping you to hide and pretend you're connecting with others? How can you connect IRL (in real life)?

PRACTICE Call a friend and meet in person.

BREATH PRAYER I am not forgotten—God calls me by name.

DAY 6

CROSSROADS

This is what the Lord says:
"Stand at the crossroads and look;
ask for the ancient paths,
ask where the good way is, and walk in it,
and you will find rest for your souls."

Jeremiah 6:16 (NIV)

One day while I was praying, the Lord told me I was at a crossroad. Just like a driver of a car needs to focus on the road ahead and not get distracted by a roadside tree, my faith would drift toward wherever my eyes were fixed. My eyes were often distracted by fears about my husband's health, our children's unprocessed emotions, and our financial struggles. The Lord said if I continued to focus on what could or should be done—or what I must have rather than what he did and was doing—I'd crash. I knew if I didn't address this, I'd become bitter and unfruitful. Slowly, I released the pain, disappointment, and unforgiveness that I built around my heart when Nick's kidneys were failing. I was learning how to still trust God while living with unanswered questions and unmet needs. You may be feeling the same way. You're looking at everything that happened and is happening to your people over generations and the terror of it all. You may ask how any of that is good. That's not the point—it wasn't good, it really wasn't. It was not God's desire for us.

What I've often heard from the Lord in prayer is, "I am with you. Walk with me." On our journeys, the Holy Spirit lovingly extends an invitation: "Whether you turn to the right or to the left, your ears will hear a voice behind you, saying, 'This is the way; walk in it'" (Isaiah 30:21 NIV). Through it all, God's unseen hand carried us. Out of the ashes of multiple disappointments, the Lord gave us over ten years of fruitful ministry in Johannesburg. I led an outreach program for teenage girls and women in Johannesburg townships. While Nick was a university professor, we served as lay pastors, and we created and ran The Well of Life, an inner healing course at our church.

As you face your own crossroad, please be compassionate with yourself and know God is gracious and patient with us. Being here today is a testimony of this reality. As we think about the state of the world and the injustice that continues, remember that perhaps our ancestors prayed, not knowing that someday we would be here alive, standing and trying to love God, ourselves, our families, and our neighbors as best we can. "These are days to return to spiritual disciplines of prayer, Bible study, fasting, gathering, worshipping. No new way. It's the ancient path." The Lord constantly speaks as we engage in these disciplines. So, create space each day to pray, listen, and walk the ancient path.

REFLECT I encourage you to ask God to show you if there are distractions by the side of the road. Is there a recurring theme, and if so, what is it, and why?

PRACTICE Hebrews 13:15 introduces a practice; "Therefore, let us offer through Jesus a continual sacrifice of praise to God, proclaiming our allegiance to his name." Today, while at your crossroad, sing or hum along to one or more Christian worship songs in your mother tongue. The practice of praise and worship helps to center God in your life and reduces stress.

BREATH PRAYER I will find true—rest for my soul.

DAY 7

SEEDS OF PROMISES

But do not ignore this one fact, beloved, that with the Lord one day is like a thousand years, and a thousand years are like one day. The Lord is not slow about his promise, as some think of slowness, but is patient with you, not wanting any to perish, but all to come to repentance.

2 PETER 3:8-9 (NRSV)

I remember a time when it was fine to be me and alive. After school, pushing shopping carts and racing them in the store parking lot. Those singing competitions with my brother, Kwame. Nana's treats of soda pop and cakes just because. Me laughing with Nana and imagining, not being frightened by my feelings and feeling that nothing would destroy me. There was no need for compulsions because they paled in comparison to knowing who I was. I had no fear about what might happen, loss or disappointment or being on my own to figure it all out. It has been a long journey for me to try to recapture this level of joy, peace, and freedom, but now it's from a different source.

The truth is we aren't expected to trust, rest, or obey by ourselves. We have a Helper and sometimes we get help from unexpected sources. South Africa has a healthy custom of shutting down entirely for the last two weeks of the year. Many people return to their ancestral family homes to celebrate what is called the Festive Season. For my family, it provided an opportunity to reflect on what took place in the past year. We remembered how God's promises came in seed form and how impatient we were to see them spring to life. We also faced temptations to believe that there was much more we could have done or could have done better.

Perhaps a similar voice inside your head sometimes accuses you of not doing more or not always being on the front lines. We may strive and strain to maintain perfection, thinking it will prevent God from losing interest in us. We may also believe we must work hard and without mistakes so we don't lose out on what God has for us. The stress of this is just as big a mistake. Our salvation is not all on us. The truth is that God has not gotten bored with us. We are not left alone hoping someone will save us. Jesus is truly Immanuel, God with us. His love is deep, wide, high, and long—and surpasses all understanding. And his promises will always be fulfilled. Jesus teaches us to grab hold of his love and grace that help us navigate through life in this country and on earth.

REFLECT Has the Lord given you seeds of promise that have germinated or been fulfilled, or seeds that need more water, to germinate or grow?

PRACTICE Post a Scripture verse in a prominent place to remind you that the Lord is with you in the waiting.

PRAYER Lord, you are faithful to keep your promises—every one of them. Help me to be still and know that you are God. I pray that you will, in an opportune time, open doors for me to impact my family, other folks, communities, and society for Christ. In Jesus' name, amen.

DAY 8

SEEDS OF TRUST

Look at the birds. They don't plant or harvest or store food in barns, for your heavenly Father feeds them. And aren't you far more valuable to him than they are?

MATTHEW 6:26

We all have painful experiences and sometimes we cry out to God for help. We struggle as we wait. The enemy sows seeds of mistrust that challenge the truth that there is always hope. Then we may frantically strive to find our way. We trust more in ourselves than God and lean on our own understanding. We have much to learn from our ancestors who experienced deep wounds and deep wonder. They waited for green sprouts, harvest, or change to come—although they couldn't see it. They battled with doubt and yet held onto the belief that this was not all there was or would ever be. They resisted the pull to hoard or consume everything. They trusted God for present and future provision.

During the decade we lived in South Africa, I believed my steps were ordered by God. But there were times when I waited and things did not happen as I wanted. I was overwhelmed trying to raise financial support to sustain the ministry to abused and unhoused women and children. I became like seed sown in poor soil. I didn't have the words to explain the bleakness I often felt. Sometimes I felt like I was coming out of winter, and spring shoots were coming up from the ground; trees were budding, but I wasn't sure they'd survive the transition.

Whether we've entered a season or moment of loss, longing, lack, or fruitfulness, we may feel some level of uncertainty. We know the seeds and trees planted but the production level is unknown, and we don't know if the fruit is edible and ready for harvest. This is where prayer, hope, trust, and faith are needed. In South Africa I witnessed miracles firsthand and ever so slowly, hope and trust grew within me. The abundance of fruit was evident in the lives of those I walked alongside. For each of us, provision and change may happen quickly or, other times, slowly, or won't be evident until months or years later. Yet when we look back, we often see the Lord's hand. Although we may doubt that we are entering a new season to hope again, it is okay to still pray "Lord, I trust and believe you are directing my steps; please help Thou my unbelief."

A WORD OF ENCOURAGEMENT In prayer I heard, "I see the fruit and the worth beyond what you know. The impact has been great. Will you trust that I'm at work in, with, and through you in a mighty way? Don't look at things from a human perspective. I'd rather one life is changed than you dance in and out of many lives. My dear one, focus is the order of the day. Focus on the few so that many will be transformed."

REFLECT What is your trust level with God?

PRAYER Lord, help me to receive your love in its many forms. Please help me to unlink love and whatever "stuff" I believe affirms that I've earned this favor. In Jesus' name, amen.

DAY 9

SEEDS OF HOPE

But blessed are those who trust in the LORD
and have made the LORD their hope and confidence.
They are like trees planted along a riverbank,
with roots that reach deep into the water.

JEREMIAH 17:7-8

When I think about home and my grandparents, I also think about the many other folks who brought gifts I missed when I wasn't paying attention. Sometimes the experiences were like water pooling on the surface of dry ground; they didn't seem to penetrate my awareness. Yet ever so slowly the water evaporated—and some of it seeped in. It began to water and nourish the seeds of hope planted long ago. These days we are in desperate need of renewed hope that helps revive our souls. Theologian Howard Thurman said,

> The movement of the Spirit of God in the hearts of men and women often calls them to act against the spirit of their times or causes them to anticipate a spirit which is yet in the making. In a moment of dedication, they are given wisdom and courage to dare a deed that challenges and to kindle a hope that inspires.

I remember moving to Johannesburg, South Africa. I was both excited and petrified at the same time. During our first month in South Africa, I found that all commitments will get tested. It started with the move into our new home. Living behind barred doors and windows was a huge adjustment. I began to experience emotional robbery. I built a figurative, internal wall that I could raise and lower at will. It was a wall around my heart that gave me the illusion of safety and emotional protection from all the uncertainty and tragedy around me. But I lost sight of much of the beauty around me. I thought I had released my expectations, fears, and disappointments, but eventually, I laid another row of bricks onto my walled heart—an attempt to create some equilibrium.

Hope returned as I released my fears to God. Linking arms with the team, we obtained the courage to dare a deed that challenged and kindle a hope that inspired. Right now, we may be experiencing the freshness of spring, the warmth of summer, the harvest of autumn, or the harshness of winter. But the seeds of hope are still being planted within us, and soon we will become like a tree planted by the riverbank. Jeremiah 17:8 tells us,

> Such trees are not bothered by the heat
> or worried by long months of drought.
> Their leaves stay green,
> and they never stop producing fruit.

A WORD OF ENCOURAGEMENT In prayer I heard, "Hold onto hope even while all else gives way. Jesus is your hope and praise. Trust me, I am not trying to wear you down nor can you deplete the strength you draw from me. Although you don't see it, you are healing and your mind is being renewed."

REFLECTION How are you praying while struggling to trust God?

PRACTICE Pray creatively: Write, draw, or take a photo that depicts the good things you're hoping for.

BREATH PRAYER Lord you are—my hope and confidence.

DAY 10

GATHERING STRAW

That same day Pharaoh told the men who made the people work, "Do not give the people straw for making clay blocks any more. Let them go and gather straw for themselves. But have them make the same number of clay blocks as before, and no less."

Exodus 5:6-8 (NLV)

Several years ago, I wept at our staff meeting. I felt exhausted, like I was swimming upstream with a heavy load on my back. I believed I had to carry the microaggressions, drama, people, and things at my own expense. I was burdened by living in a time when many deny the facts about past and present-day racism and the impact of systemic oppression on us. But we know the truth. As I prayed, the story of those enslaved in Egypt came to mind. In Exodus 5, after Moses and Aaron plead with Pharoah to give the Israelites a three-day reprieve to go into the wilderness to worship God, Pharaoh responds, "I will not give you straw. You go and get straw for yourselves where you can find it. But you will not work any less than before" (Exodus 5:10-11 NLV). The people went out and gathered what they could of the dry byproduct of the harvested grain or other material to use for straw. They were also commanded to "finish your full day's work as you did when there was straw." The people were asked, "Why have you not made as many clay blocks yesterday or today as you made before?" (Exodus 3:14 NLV). Pharoah and his overseers knew the answer to this question. They were trying to gaslight the people.

We may hold beliefs that exist like a seed, soil, or straw. Below the surface of our lives, we may find rubble, weeds, noise, temptations, and lies. My parents' divorce planted a lie in me. My father loved me, but his leaving so early in my life meant I wasn't sure what it was like to have a father who was consistently present for me. This created a distorted belief about God the Father. I often felt God was like Pharaoh, refusing to hear my legitimate needs and concerns while demanding that I make bricks without straw. Some of us have felt that God is like a hard taskmaster refusing to set us free. As we engage in spiritual formation practices such as meditating on the character of Jesus in the Bible, the Holy Spirit draws us closer to the Lord, who uncovers and addresses our concerns. We learn that God is not Pharoah. He is Father to the fatherless, defender of widows—this is God, whose dwelling is holy. God places the lonely in families; he sets the prisoners free and gives them new life. The Lord will bring us out of metaphorical Egypt time and time again and will continuously nourish us. Beloved, Jesus the Son has set you free indeed. So let's walk in greater freedom.

A WORD OF ENCOURAGEMENT In prayer I heard, "I am always at work in ways you do not see. Let me care for you. Slow down; I am not Pharaoh demanding that you perform. It's you who believes you need to prove to others that what you have to offer is of quality. You are already loved."

REFLECT Do you have any distortions about God's character?

PRACTICE Meditate on the character of Jesus in the Bible.

PRAYER Lord, I pray right now to release my distortions. Help me see who you are and how you see and feel about me. In Jesus' name, amen.

PART 2

The Soil of Your Story

Days 11-21

Let your roots grow down into him,
and let your lives be built on him.

Colossians 2:7

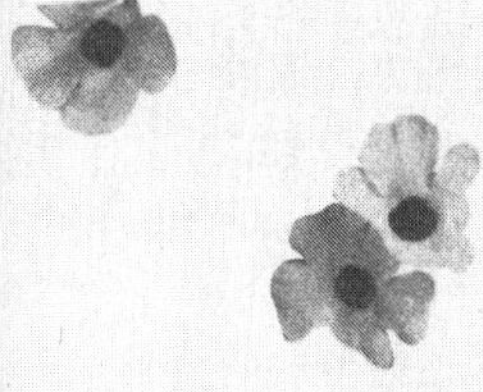

DAY 11

THE CONDITION OF THE SOIL

But if a field bears thorns and thistles, it is useless. The farmer will soon condemn that field and burn it.

HEBREWS 6:8

Although we often evaluate the seed when its plants become visible, the condition of the soil, the environment, and the time seeds spend in the soil directly correlate with what's produced.

So the ground must be prepared, and this starts with us. Depending on the season, some of us will be called to lie fallow for a bit. We are like land that is plowed but for a season is left without crops. This allows the soil to recover and become fertile ground again. Others of us need to cease restless activism and lie low instead. Still others will invite Jesus to break up the fallow ground because it's time to sow seed. At some point we will be ready to dig or till the soil. We can then take a hard look at the past experiences and environments that have left depleted soil, weeds, or debris that we must attend to. Other times we feel we are on solid ground, then a racist event occurs, and the ground suddenly shifts. Somehow, we believe we can still grow and thrive despite the ground in which we are planted. But we test the soil and find it has too much sand, silt, or debris to grow anything healthy.

Each of us is at a different stage of the growth process in different areas of our lives. Each area needs specific care because the soil or environment that we live in and through affects the spirit, mind, and body. We may be in places or with certain people, and our bodies tense up and our breathing is shallow or rapid. We may struggle to stay in the present moment while our bodies are trying to communicate something is off. In response to racial trauma and bias, our bodies may react in several ways. We may freeze up or flee by denying the harm. We may fight but unproductively or try to prevent further harm by fawning to placate our abusers, or we may forfeit our connection to our community.

When I became a Christian, I believed that I had miraculously gotten over the pain and racial trauma of being bused to all-White schools. But this wasn't true. There were many moments of frustration when I berated myself because I "should have it all together and be over it." Sometime later I realized that my past experiences weren't just memories but trauma that continued to impact my life. Yet Jesus offers healing and so much more. The grounding we long for happens more profoundly as we focus on the one true source of security. Psalm 46 tells us,

> God [you are] our refuge and strength,
> an ever-present help in trouble.
> Therefore we will not fear, though the earth give way
> and the mountains fall into the heart of the sea,
> though its waters roar and foam
> and the mountains quake with their surging.
> (Psalm 46:1-3 NIV)

As we consider the condition of our land or soil, Hebrews 6:7 tells us,

> When the ground soaks up the falling rain and bears a
> good crop for the farmer, it has God's blessing.

Ultimately God fully heals and blesses us and is the solid ground upon which we can safely stand.

REFLECTION What is the condition of the past and present soil you've built your life on?

Write how you will attend to what surfaced from today.

PRACTICE There are practices that help when unwanted memories and emotions surface. When we are quiet and pray, we can do a body scan where we listen for stress or any pain points in our bodies and minds. What may surface are things we need to tend to. Sometimes we learn of the source of our stress and often after this, we pray we can release it. This practical grounding technique, in addition to patience and self-compassion, offers stress relief and regulates our emotions.

PRAYER Dear Lord, I take this time to set myself apart so I can hear from you. I race from one thing to another with little time to stop and reflect on the state of my heart or the state of my life. I choose to slow down today and do a body scan to listen for the Holy Spirit revealing what needs to be released so my roots can grow deeper into you. In Jesus' name, amen.

DAY 12

TOXIC SOIL

When you walk through the fire of oppression,
you will not be burned up;
the flames will not consume you.

Isaiah 43:2

Many of our stories include—to varying degrees—words spoken and actions taken that caused us harm. Just as a careless word is like a spark that sets a forest alight, abuse or neglect in any form profoundly impacts our lives. It does not matter the degree of verbal, physical, neglectful, sexual, and spiritual abuse; racism; colorism; gaslighting; sidelining; or power and political dynamics. All of these are like the toxic soil that remains after a burning. We may struggle to fully embrace Christ's love and sacrifice because of the damage done. We may even have an existential crisis and question life's meaning and purpose. Racism, abuse, and neglect silence our voices and choices. This makes it hard to ask for help, and it can feel unsafe to confront harm. It's one thing to face interpersonal and systemic racism in the world, but it's more hurtful in our families and communities. And when the church inflicts spiritual abuse and manipulation, this jeopardizes our ability to live and remember well.

A pathway to healing racial trauma starts with cycling through feeling unsafe, feeling safe enough, and then attending to the harm. But you must go at your own pace. Healing will follow but by its own timeline and process. We may leave a situation so we can heal. Although we may be tempted to also jettison our faith, we don't need to leave Jesus, our first love.

I once held a position where I had interactions with coworkers that left me confused. I learned that if I took a pause, I felt like I could breathe, freely exhaling and inhaling. Despite the gaslighting I endured, I realized that I wasn't blowing things out of proportion. Nor did I have a hard time asking folks to do stuff, including asking God. Yes, there were times when I was all up in my head and trying to figure out how to leave my job. I stressed over it and lost sleep. But I also found that I had folk in my life who were a lot more compassionate than I thought. They were God's surprise provision as I moved on to my next job.

We may not believe or feel it's true, but Jesus the Good Shepherd finds the wandering, confused sheep—the one kicked out of the fold or trying to survive in toxic soil. Jesus heals and helps us to feel safe enough again. When we're ready, we and the Lord can attend to the harm. But we will also need safe-enough people to love, pray, and be empathetic witnesses to help us process and address our pain. We may cycle back and forth between denial, anger, bargaining, grieving, and speaking the truth about how the harm affects us. Deep healing can occur as we weep over what was lost and stolen.

A WORD OF ENCOURAGEMENT As you walk through the fire of pain and oppression with Jesus, you are not consumed. Instead, transformation is happening incrementally, and soon you begin to walk in your true identity as a worthy child of God.

REFLECT How have you been harmed personally or institutionally (be specific about who and how)?

PRACTICE Further process your thoughts and feelings with a trusted friend, pastor, or therapist.

BREATH PRAYER Jesus heals and helps me—I will not be consumed.

DAY 13

THE FOOTPATH

A farmer went out to plant some seeds.
As he scattered them across his field,
some seeds fell on a footpath, and
the birds came and ate them.

MATTHEW 13:3-4

On the footpath the ground is dry, hard gravel or asphalt, so seeds struggle to take root. Jesus explains how the seeds that fell on the footpath represent those who hear the message about the kingdom and don't understand it. "Then the evil one comes and snatches away the seed that was planted in their hearts" (Matthew 13:19). The enemy also snatches away any positive words spoken over us. Truths about our identity as a BIPOC child of God and the calling on our life may be replaced with lies. We are seen as a problem or as incompetent. Our names are mispronounced; our stories are ignored or unheard. In life and in our work we may long for promotion, but again it is denied. We walk through life and at any moment we may have an encounter where we're called out of our name.

My earliest memory of seed falling on the footpath was when I had to speak in front of my primary school class. I was one of few Black girls in the class. I knew I had good things to say and deserved to speak, but when I saw the sea of snickering White faces, I became terrified and fumbled over my words. My shame grew as those who followed me performed much better. I longed for the congratulation or consolation that never came.

This is when my performance anxiety first surfaced. Later in life, many times I did perform well, and the affirmations came, but they fell on the footpath and were also quickly snatched away. This lasted for decades. I carried feelings of shame from being told that I was "less than" because I was a Black girl growing up in poverty. A part of me feared that I deserved punishment just because everything about me was wrong. Intellectually I knew it wasn't true. But how do we grow in an environment and season where there's so much that threatens and demeans the *imago Dei* (image of God) in us and those who look like us?

What I learned is that holding onto the truth of who we really are requires diligence. When we try to heal or save ourselves, it won't work or last. This lesson is also my encouragement: We can stop and exchange our burden for his. When we know God is sovereign, the internal pressure to impulsively do something, anything is removed. The Lord heals our battered hearts and within it places good soil and seed. Pride, fear, or other things are cut away. Then slowly we start to relax and soak up the growing peace and freedom found within and around us every day.

A WORD OF ENCOURAGEMENT In prayer I heard, "Remember my great love. You are considered and not ignored. Trust in that love and walk in the spirit of love, power, and a sound mind. I console and grant peace to your heart and strength to your frame. Although you don't see it, your small and large acts and very presence have an impact on those around you."

REFLECT Did your seed fall on the footpath? If so, who or what was the enemy that snatched it up? Do you want to retrieve what was stolen from you or lost?

BREATH PRAYER I am loved by God—who created melanin.

DAY 14

ROCKY PLACES

Some [seed] fell on rocky places, where it did not have much soil.
It sprang up quickly, because the soil was shallow.
But when the sun came up, the plants were scorched,
and they withered because they had no root.

MATTHEW 13:5-6 (NIV)

Some of our lives began in a very rocky place. We now want our roots to grow down into Jesus, but this is a struggle, and we may not know why. Past and current environments and experiences affect our lives. In moments along the way, caregivers and others failed us. We've also dealt with racist people and systems that communicate that healing and forward movement or justice are impossible. These obstacles cause turmoil and strife in our life and relationships. Although these connections may be rocky, we want something to grow there. And so, we need to confront and remove these rocks or stumbling blocks.

Work was a stumbling block for me. I can hardly remember when I wasn't working. I officially became a worker when I was twelve and our city had a special jobs program for inner city kids. Because of work, I didn't fully enjoy my youth. Growing up, some of us may have been the competent and strong ones who helped in the family business, were put in positions of authority, or seemed older than we really were. We became responsible for things like carrying the cares of our family. For many BIPOC children in America and around the world, life involves performing and responding to others. And then we grow into BIPOC adults who are told we can carry even more. But this is not sustainable. Our arms are growing weary and our shoulders slump.

Our work or ministry may have started with a clear vision, then it morphed into something we hadn't signed up for. Perhaps there was a power struggle, and it felt like success or failure rested solely on our heads. Then God reminds us that we were never meant to carry this weight all on our own. We must learn how to release our successes or failures to God. We may revolt after realizing the work, ministry, and "running on the treadmill" needed to come to a glorious end. But we can still ask the Lord if a re-vision or return to the original concept should happen instead. God can do above and beyond what we can think of or ask. Even in shallow or rocky soil, God can plant seeds of his love and grace that grow. Take a moment and consider the tenacity of his seed. Nothing stands in its way. This seed is the kind of faith, trust, and tenacity we want and can all pray for.

A WORD OF ENCOURAGEMENT In prayer I heard, "Sustainability comes from me not you. You need help from me and from other people. I am leading you on a path where there will be a bench to sit and reset."

REFLECT Where has your seed fallen on shallow soil with underlying rock? How have you pushed through in the past?

PRACTICE Take a walk and choose a rock to remind you that Christ is now the rock on which you stand.

BREATH PRAYER I welcome the love—and grace of Christ Jesus.

DAY 15

AMONG THORNS

Other seeds fell among thorns that grew up and choked out the tender plants.

MATTHEW 13:7

Despite the fact that I am a follower of Christ, I still am impacted by the struggles of being a BIPOC in this country. The truth of the matter is that it's difficult to look at all the damage done by racism and other harms. Past and present experiences of racism come in many forms. Often, these are interpersonal and systemic attempts to shut us up. Our voices are unwelcomed, ignored; our ideas aren't taken seriously. We may have learned to deny the trauma or to respond in unhelpful ways to try to protect ourselves. So, like a beautiful rose, we may bear thorns that warn others to watch their step. Some of us question whether the shield of faith is large enough to cover and protect us from the flaming arrows of the enemy, or even from thorns and thistles.

I've certainly experienced this after being silenced at such a young age. I felt my voice was not to be raised above the din of angry White parents and sometimes children. My Black parents wanted so desperately to believe that being bused to an all-White school would result in a better education for me. However, in my classes I often sat in silence while my fear mounted. Back then I didn't know the Lord Jesus could meet me in the middle of it. Like me, you may need lots of prayer and support to be honest with the Lord, yourself, and others about what you have or are experiencing. We all need to intentionally and verbally make a choice to trust God with our heart.

Although we may not see an immediate change in our situations, Jesus stands with us. Perhaps he has come when we felt silenced or isolated like the woman at the well. Maybe, like Zacchaeus, we're clearly sinners, but Jesus still engages with us. He forgives and calls us by name and deems us daughter, son, or friend, and he tells us, "I'm going to spend this evening dining at your house." Like seed sown among thorns, we may feel our fruitfulness will forever be impaired. Despite our limited imaginations, the Lord always has a way of restoring us—and more. Isaiah 55:13 says,

> Where once there were thorns, cypress trees will grow.
> Where nettles grew, myrtles will sprout up.
> These events will bring great honor to the Lord's name;
> they will be an everlasting sign of his power and love.

In Scriptures like this we find comfort and reassurance. Even today we may see a little bit more clearly and witness a small shoot breaking through the soil.

A WORD OF ENCOURAGEMENT In prayer I heard, "Because you can't immediately see, you discount that I'm at work and that there is indeed a shifting, growth, and expansion happening. Do what is in front of you; one by one trust me to give all you need to accomplish my purposes and plans. As it is in heaven it shall be on earth. Walk closely with my Spirit. Dwell in my sanctuary, be at home with me. What I have is beyond compare. I have all you need. There is no lack of abundance, grace, love, favor. Trust me."

REFLECT Wherever you find yourself today, consider what may help you to keep your eyes on God, your Healer and Provider.

LISTENING PRAYER Lord, remind me once again of your faithfulness. Forgive and strengthen me so that I can keep the shield of faith by my side, ready to hold it up to extinguish any arrows of the enemy. In Jesus' name, amen.

DAY 16

GRAINS OF RESPONSIBILITY

Take my yoke upon you. Let me teach you, because I am humble and gentle at heart, and you will find rest for your souls. For my yoke is easy to bear, and the burden I give you is light."

MATTHEW 11:29-30

I remember when I felt the work of the ministry was drifting off course, but I didn't ask for help. I sat, overly responsible and frustrated about how the story that I told myself led to feeling this was normal. To change course, I needed to see and tell the truth to myself and grieve the loss of focus, energy, and money. I laid down my false pride that said, "I know" or "I should have known." I confessed to the Lord that I didn't know what I was doing. I prayed, "God, show me your will and your way where my faith and works matter." I found the Holy Spirit always brings comfort and the truth. These are so needed when we experience interpersonal and systemic racism, and the question is who's responsible for what.

Many of us were taught human interactions in simple cause-and-effect terms. We wondered what we did or had not done that caused the harm done to us. Now as adults, we continue to operate in the same way. If we are angry, someone else caused it or we need to fix it; if someone's mad at us, we must be to blame. Some of us feel that the other has no right to be upset. We tend to respond in four ways. We're under-responsible, we're over-responsible, we blame, or we recognize. Each reaction has underlying feelings of anger, sadness, and fear.

We who are under-responsible may have difficulty showing our strong, competent side. We sometimes find ourselves in situations where we are marginalized or exploited because we don't or can't take a strong stand. We wait for others to hopefully read our minds and may become angry when folk don't. In my life, I carried over-responsibility because I wanted things to be done and to look a certain way. I had a hard time asking people to do what they were responsible for. I'm not a doormat or a people pleaser, but I had to learn to be clear about what I needed. We who are over-responsible may try to advise, rescue, and take over—especially when there has been a racist incident. We're seen as always having it together, and caring for ourselves is rare. Somehow we believe we have the superpower to make people change. We are the saviors—not called by God, but motivated by our need to be needed. This is tiring, and we may be angry about this. Those of us who are blamers hold other folks responsible for our own feelings and actions. We respond to anxiety with anger and fighting. But we don't have to go to our familiar responses when a racist incident happens. Those who recognize the truth and feelings like anger and feeling stuck can better understand who's responsible, including our role in it.

It is essential that we have healthy relationships where we can receive help to see what is real and true, and how to implement the three P's: pause, pray, and proceed. First, we pause and look for patterns: Who's over-responsible, who's under-responsible, and who's blaming or recognizing and acknowledging the truth. Then we pray and listen for who did what, when, and what triggers were pushed in us. In codependency support groups, the four W's also help us to discern who caused it, who won't change it, who won't control it, and who is acknowledging it.

Answering these questions helps us to take small steps toward healing: Under-responsible ones can speak up or take full responsibility for a small thing. Over-responsible ones can reveal a need for help. Blamers can see options—even ones we may not want to take. Finally, like those who acknowledge it, we can pray some more for God to inform whether a burden or grain of responsibility is ours to carry. But most importantly, we must know that the Lord will help us to bear it.

REFLECT What is your go-to when it comes to responsibility? How might you begin to change this?

PRACTICE Pray while using your hands to symbolically wipe off your shoulders to represent removing the burden of responsibility that you carry that God has not asked you to bear.

LISTENING PRAYER Lord, in this moment, I listen for you to reveal the burdens I'm carrying. And now I ask you to exchange my burden for yours, knowing that your yoke is easy and your burden light. I give you the burden of fear, anger, grief, and all else that weighs me down—the racism and the systemic oppression. I open my hands and extend them to you, and as I turn my hands over palms facing downward, I release my wounds and burdens to you. Now with palms facing upward I welcome hope, joy, and wonder. In Jesus' name, amen.

DAY 17

THE ROOTS OF THOUGHTS AND FEELINGS

Don't copy the behavior and customs of this world, but let God transform you into a new person by changing the way you think. Then you will learn to know God's will for you, which is good and pleasing and perfect.

ROMANS 12:2

Growing up in Boston and bused to majority-White schools, I was shamed and faced unrest. I learned to follow all the rules: some instituted by my parents, but most by society. I kept silent about the racial trauma I experienced in those schools. I went into hiding about my pain. Later, I believed no one wanted to listen to or read what I had to say anyway. Later in life, I didn't send out writing submissions because of fear my work would be rejected or stolen. I went with the status quo and didn't try to do anything deep or different in my writing. I was reluctant to dream, hope, or believe that things could change.

Like me, you may sometimes forget that you have an adversary, a thief, who doesn't want you to heal and grow. So you believe lies about yourself. These pretenses and temptations continue to affect how we now perceive God, ourselves, and others. First Corinthians 10:13 (NIV) says, "No temptation has overtaken you except what is common to mankind. And God is faithful; he will not let you be tempted beyond what you can bear. But when you are tempted, he will also provide a way out so that you can endure it."

We must be wary of the temptation to think that our pain and brokenness are unique or insurmountable. This is not true. Many practices may help when we struggle with the fruit of troubling memories, thoughts, emotions, and feelings. These widely accepted grounding techniques, including deep breathing, offer practical coping skills. Science has shown these may help reorient our thought life from fixating on the negative to the more positive. Yet Jesus offers this and so much more. As we stop and look, then listen to our heart, what is it saying? We learn how our thoughts and feelings deeply affect us. But we can take every random or intentional thought, feeling, or word to Jesus and ask him what he thinks about it and how we are to respond. We can "demolish arguments and every pretension that sets itself up against the knowledge of God and we take captive every thought to make it obedient to Christ" (2 Corinthians 10:5 NIV).

Sometimes we discover our feelings are masking unmet needs. Once uncovered, we can pray about how these needs can or can't be met. Over time we find that God is changing the way we think and feel—and what we believe about Jesus, ourselves, others, and, often, our situations. We start to appreciate tiny moments of joy that help rewire the neural pathways in our brain where our thoughts often skew toward the negative. Increasingly our thoughts and feelings align with Philippians 4:6-7, "Don't worry about anything; instead, pray about everything. Tell God what you need, and thank him for all he has done. Then you will experience God's peace, which exceeds anything we can understand. His peace will guard your hearts and minds as you live in Christ Jesus."

A WORD OF ENCOURAGEMENT In prayer I heard, "My grace and power are made perfect in weakness. Over time as you continue to follow my lead, you are empowered to confront distortions. I continually impart strength and help transform you into a new person by changing the way you think and what you believe."

REFLECT Stop and look. Listen to your heart. What is it saying? Ask God to help you take every thought captive and make it subject to Christ. What is the Lord saying about it?

PRACTICE Write out an honest prayer using the Psalms as a model.

LISTENING PRAYER Lord, help me to take every concerning thought, feeling, and action captive and make them subject to Christ. Please show me the truth and the way to respond as you transform me to be more like Jesus. In his name, amen.

DAY 18

PULLING THE WEEDS OF SHAME

Instead of shame and dishonor,
you will enjoy a double share of honor.
You will possess a double portion of prosperity in your land,
and everlasting joy will be yours.

Isaiah 61:7

Healing began when I became honest about what happened, getting in touch with the pain, then forgiving and allowing the Lord to heal that part of me that still whispered, "You aren't good enough." The Samaritan woman also had a profound encounter with Jesus and the truth. He told her, "'Go call your husband and come back.' The woman said, 'I have no husband'" (John 4:16-17 NLV). Too often, rather than telling the truth and getting healed, we try to hide our shame, but the shame eventually affects how we view ourselves and others. We have lives full of "should" and "ought to," and when confronted with our own limitations, we experience shame. We minimize the truth rather than deal with reality. We may live a double life, we code-switch. There is a big difference between who we are at home and who we are in public or who we are on the inside and who we are on the outside. We may not understand shame and label it by its manifestations, such as fear, confusion, rage, indifference, or the other person's fault.

It's been said that shame tells us who and what we aren't while God tells us who and what we are. Shame is often confused with guilt, which is an emotion that arises when we have in fact done something wrong. Shame says it is not what we have done that is wrong but it who we are that is wrong. We believe it is better to hide or disappear to keep people from knowing our secret self. And certainly, we do not deserve to partake of the life-giving water Jesus offers. It's been said that "shame can hold us back, hold us down and keep us staring at our feet."

We've climbed into many wells over the years in search of water. But, like the Samaritan woman, our thirst was not quenched by drops of water. We still hoped someone would tell us that we're okay. Jesus said to the woman at the well and to us, "Let me give you water that will cause you never to thirst again. The water that I give will satisfy, welling up to eternal life" (see John 4:14). Instead of continuing to hide behind a veil of shame, isolated from her community, the Samaritan woman grabbed hold of his water and drank deeply.

The woman's story is a subtle but meaningful metaphor; she now has a new source and a new means of getting her needs met. She leaves her water jar and goes into the town to spread the good news that the Christ has come. "She said to the men, 'Come and see a Man Who told me everything I ever did! Can this be the Christ?' . . . They said to the woman, 'Now we believe!'" (John 4:28-29, 42 NLV). Jesus restores the Samaritan woman's life and relationships within her community. The Lord does the same for us. He removes our shame, reveals our purpose, and honors us right where we are.

A WORD OF ENCOURAGEMENT Although the adversary may try to bind us with guilt and shame, go to prayer and acknowledge any sin or distortion about what you did or who you are as a person. Ask for forgiveness for the sin or freedom from the lies you believe about yourself. The Holy Spirit will establish the truth within your heart that you are forgiven and loved, and I pray that like the Samaritan woman, you may receive a double portion of honor and blessing in your land.

REFLECT Are there racist people or others who shame you, or do you diminish and shame yourself for not "measuring up"? If so, how?

LISTENING PRAYER Abba Father, today I choose to no longer believe the lie that I'm [name the ways shame has defined you]. Please sever this lie from my mind, heart, and body. I now wait to hear your special word affirming who I am in you: [Listen for what God reveals]. Thank you, Lord Jesus, for freedom and for help to fully accept and live out my true identity as your child. In Jesus' name, amen.

ON BEING

You are joined to Christ Who was raised from the dead. This is so we may be what God wants us to be. Our lives are to give fruit for Him.

Romans 7:4 (NLV)

In my youth, I sporadically attended Pentecostal churches where the body was an integral part of worship. The shouting, wailing, dancing, and stomping were all expressions of worship as the body and the Holy Spirit were engaged. I saw how the Holy Spirit could inhabit hearts and inform thoughts. I could embrace all of who I was as the Holy Spirit met me in the places where I struggled or was in pain. My doubts didn't matter. The reality of life, redemption, and healing was clear, and deep down in my bones I knew my Redeemer lives, that Jesus is real.

However, during and after high school and college, things changed, and I spent years content in the belief that my body was my own and I could do with it as I pleased. Although the Bible says that our bodies are temples of the Holy Spirit, holding that truth and tension was difficult because our bodies want what they want. The apostle Paul talks about this internal struggle in Romans 7:15 (NIV), "I do not understand what I do. For what I want to do I do not do, but what I hate I do." We may not be doing well in every way, but we don't feel strong in body and soul.

Like Adam and Eve banished from the garden, we fight to return when God has made a way through the life, death, and resurrection of his Son. We are told we also can invite Jesus in to sup or dine with us. Yet if we were honest, on some level, we have questions: Will he really want to fellowship with me? How do I invite him in? What is he going to do or think? I think of the times when I have invited a special guest over, and the first thing I do is clean my house—at least, the most visible rooms. And I keep the guest away from certain areas of the house. Initially we accepted Jesus and invited him into the mess in our life. We allowed him to stay, but over the years we've built onto the house, and now more rooms are off limits. Jesus is only welcomed in the cleaner or slightly disheveled rooms. So the notion of allowing Jesus to come into all the rooms of our heart and allowing him to declutter, rearrange, or renovate may be intimidating. But Jesus wants to see every space. Yet as with any other guest, we fear ridicule and judgment, and we certainly do not want an offer to clean it up. But we can invite Jesus into all the rooms to clean up the mess. It does not matter whether the room was trashed long ago or last week. He may reveal how he is at work in us to heal and restore us of past or current wounds.

But will we invite him in? The world tells us to be strong, suck it up, get over it. It's not a big deal; look at me, I got over it; do what you're told; it's better to look good than to feel good. These rules are so ingrained that we need to renounce them to follow the new and living way the Lord has for us. If we change ourselves for someone else, we become invisible. Sometimes as a BIPOC in this country, we forget or have a hard time grasping this because so often we grin and bear it in our own strength. The apostle Paul goes on to ask who will save him from this. It is Jesus. "Therefore, I urge you, brothers and sisters, in view of God's mercy, to offer your bodies as a living sacrifice, holy and pleasing to God—this is your true and proper worship" (Romans 12:1 NIV).

A WORD OF ENCOURAGEMENT We are on a wonderful and sometimes frightening journey. Yet Emmanuel God is with us, and we're being changed by an ongoing process of sanctification. We're moving from glory to glory. Sometimes we get this, and other times we struggle to hold on. Yet we move inch by inch and step by step, being transformed. Our histories and the stories of our ancestors to the present are significant. Still we're becoming who we were truly meant to be. Yes, this means being more like Christ, but it also means being more like who we are as BIPOC children of God. We can live, tell, and write about our whole, true story. Regardless of the soil we're in, we were fearfully and wonderfully made to be with and bear fruit for our God.

REFLECT Consider some of the good and great things about you and your community's style of prayer, praise, and worship.

PRACTICE Sit in a chair and gently rock from side to side, or back and forward. This may help reconnect with your body, calm you, and regulate your nervous system.

BREATH PRAYER Lord may my body and mind be—as strong and well as my soul is.

DAY 20

SUSTENANCE

Certainly there were many needy widows in Israel in Elijah's time, when the heavens were closed for three and a half years, and a severe famine devastated the land. Yet Elijah was not sent to any of them.

LUKE 4:25-26

After I became a lay pastor and counselor at our home church, things took a surprising turn. A member of the church handed over an eight-bedroom house to open Malibongwe Mother and Child Haven, a transitional home for unhoused and abused mothers and children. During the months of renovation, the buzz of my cell phone caused me to bolt upright in bed, partly delirious as I grabbed the phone, only to hear the live-in groundskeeper tell me of yet another attempted break-in. Those repeated disruptions led to increased fear, stress, and a sense of powerlessness that would wash over me and our team. I knew God was in control, but I oversaw the project. It was a stressful period. I began to question if the move to South Africa and leading the project was a mistake.

In Luke 4:26 Jesus recalls how Elijah "was sent instead to a foreigner—a widow of Zarephath in the land of Sidon." The full story about this powerful prophet of God and the vulnerable widow and single mother is found in 1 Kings 17:8-24. This story is a powerful illustration of the ways God invites us to risk—and the way he may use our relationships to expose the parts of ourselves that need help and healing. The story starts with Elijah, the man of God, appointed to speak reform and judgment to a corrupt king. Elijah is on the run. God instructs Elijah to go to meet the widow who would provide food.

If we look over the breadth of Scripture, God's plan is for us to engage with other folks, who may offer us sustenance. Sometimes we receive this as we lead and other times as we follow and still other times, we do both. However, if we are leading or following and have issues with authority, we may miss out on the help we each can offer. We may either react in open rebellion against authority figures or, because we feel it's too risky, we don't speak the truth to power, nor do we trust ourselves or others. Some of us may engage in passive-aggression or manipulative behaviors to get our needs across. Others fear retaliation, so it's difficult to get us to say what we really need, and this may result in much confusion. Some may even lash out in anger when we feel our needs are diminished or shamed, or we may openly retaliate. At the same time, some of us do not know what we need because we've never had the chance to express our own hearts' cries.

Although I was at risk of permanently walling myself off during those early days in Johannesburg, I was reminded that the Holy Spirit would lead me into all truth. This meant the Spirit knew all truth, not me. I learned to moderate my expectation that people would respond in a specific way. As I waited, I faced loss, fear, and disappointment. I prayed for grace and more grace to lead and to follow with a heart to serve wherever the Lord would take me. Jesus freed me to give and receive love and help from him and mentors from the community who walked with the families and with me. The spiritual, emotional, and material support helped the families and the ministry to thrive. On some level, we will all face difficulties even as the Lord is leading and we are following. But our Lord offers sustenance to equip us to work and serve in the field we are called to.

REFLECT Are you willing to lead or follow even if you don't have a map? In what field are you called to serve, tend, and harvest?

PRACTICE Create a playlist of songs that remind you to rest, play, and receive God's sustenance.

LISTENING PRAYER Lord, please show me my wrong turns or the vows of self-protection I made rather than relying on your direction and protection. Today I welcome all you offer me. In Jesus' name, amen.

DAY 21

SEEDS OF WOUNDS AND WONDER

Rejoice with those who rejoice;
mourn with those who mourn.

Romans 12:15 (NIV)

While growing up, I learned to categorize things as all good or all bad. The truth is that we live our lives in moments, days, weeks, months, seasons, and years. Through it all we will experience wounds and wonder. Most of us were never taught how to navigate through life when both occur simultaneously. So we swing from one to the other, or one pole minimizes the other—and yet the Lord is present with us. Yet it's a great help if there are folk in our lives to connect with, help, and even model how to live in the tension of wounds and wonder. They can also make and hold space for us as we swing from one pole to the other. Sometimes we can be myopic, focusing solely on what isn't going well or the pain that causes us to anticipate the same in the future. Ecclesiastes 3:11 reminds us that God has made everything beautiful for its own time. This is why we take time to reflect on the past and present, and to pray and listen about the future.

Once in prayer I heard the Lord say, "Sometimes the need for a word is more about wanting a guarantee to stave off fear that something won't happen. Is it less about encouragement and more about control?" Do you want a vision for the next season of your life when what you need to focus on is now? There is a danger of getting a word in prayer that closes out other things. Sometimes, I get a general word, then I keep circling around the meaning. It's easy to get foggy when I simply need to pray for the Holy Spirit to reveal and confirm through the Word what is true and what I really want and need. When I started to unpack my past with my counselor, I realized that for my mind to be renewed or healed, any conformity to the world's quick fixes needed to be broken.

At many times in our lives, we'll need to sow anyway, even though the ground is hard. We've been disappointed and hurt so often that to feel more is almost unbearable. Then our wounds can suppress our passion and dampen our hearts. We may bury our feelings under our addictions, compulsions, and endless scrolling on social media. But this may cause us to forget how to feel genuinely excited. And when our godly passions get killed, so do our imaginations. Why wonder about a future given the past track record? What does it take to prepare the ground for sowing and to water and protect the seed all the way to healthy plants that produce a harvest to feed many? We need to know that the wounds and wonder have contributed to who we are today. In a safe-enough space we can learn to openly share how the wounds of racial trauma affect us. We may also begin to see how glimmers of light and love shone along the way, shimmers of hope and wonder. All of these remind us that the Lord was and is always near.

A WORD OF ENCOURAGEMENT Look for those transcendent moments, often small and simple invitations to pray, weep, praise, laugh, lament, sing, and play. Like a surprise view of the sea, an unexpected gift, a dance, a glance, a prophetic word that shimmers with God's truth, a reprieve, laughter, release, a victory in court, and stories of BIPOC hope and joy.

REFLECT In this season your life, how are you experiencing wounds and wonder simultaneously?

BREATH PRAYER Holy Spirit bring me—into all truth.

PART 3

Weeds Among the Wheat

Days 22-32

The Kingdom of Heaven is like a farmer who planted good seed in his field. But that night as the workers slept, his enemy came and planted weeds among the wheat, then slipped away. When the crop began to grow and produce grain, the weeds also grew.

The farmer's workers went to him and said, "Sir, the field where you planted that good seed is full of weeds! Where did they come from?"

"An enemy has done this!" the farmer exclaimed.

MATTHEW 13:24-28

DAY 22

UNCOVERED

The time is coming when everything
that is covered up will be revealed,
and all that is secret will be made known to all.

LUKE 12:2

When we are in denial, we aren't paying attention to or don't want to look at what is real. Sometimes we think if we ignore it, a problem will go away—or maybe it doesn't really exist. But denial cannot change the truth of our history or our current stories. Denial is like a mask that covers the trauma that remains. As we heal from racial trauma, we must look at it square in the face with Jesus. To remain in denial, we are not facing the fullness of our life. Yet no one can force us out of denial. At various points we may have been challenged to do so, yet it can feel overwhelming in many ways. Denial keeps us locked in pain; fear tell us that looking at reality will cause us to return to that state. However, we now have many resources at our disposal. Jesus promises to never leave us nor forsake us. So the challenge is to take that first step and ask Jesus to accompany us as we look at all the things that we've been running from. We may wonder why God didn't do something then. This is a question to pray about.

Although I didn't want to look at things when I did, I saw I was going down a road leading me further away from God, myself, my family, and my friends. In my twenties, being involved with a substance abuser and feeling devastated, I had no choice but to look at the road that I had traveled down. I landed on a road where I was easily plucked up because the ground of relationships was toxic and unproductive. The seeds that managed to fall to that ground laid barren or became weeds. I firmly believe my mom prayed for my mask of denial to be removed. I had to choose to leave the relationship or let things stay as they were. Thankfully I heard God calling me to more life, grace, and peace. This included setting aside the mask I wore as well as who I was behind the mask. After the uncovering, I realized the truth of my life and relationships. I learned I couldn't heal the man or myself. Eventually I fully surrendered my life to Jesus, the One who can heal.

Although we've carried a lot—and we did what we knew how to do with the tools that we had at the time—now is an opportunity to begin to truly see. We may need to come out of denial again and again. But with the eyes of love, God gazes upon us and is committed to our healing and discipleship. By the Spirit of God, we are blessed and empowered to stand each day.

A WORD OF ENCOURAGEMENT In prayer I heard, "Begin and end the day with a Scripture meditation that sets the tone for the day and orients your attention on me. Because I've laid out the path already, there's no need to cut brush and create a new way. I am the way, the truth and life. Follow and walk with me, keep your eyes on me to not become distracted. Ask me where I am in a particular situation. If I'm not in it or am doing something else, I'll tell you."

REFLECT What are some things that have been covered up that the Lord is calling you to bring into the light?

PRACTICE Take a few minutes to listen or sing a worship song that encourages as God covers you.

BREATH PRAYER Wherever the Spirit of the Lord is—there is liberty.

DAY 23

SEEDS OF SAFETY

The Lord *is my shepherd;*
I have all that I need.
He lets me rest in green meadows;
he leads me beside peaceful streams.
He renews my strength.
He guides me along right paths,
bringing honor to his name.

Psalm 23:1-3

The first place where I felt safe enough to share my story was in therapy. There were few Black or Brown Christian therapists back then, so it felt like a big risk. Perhaps it was Dr. Effie's immigrant background, but this larger-than-life Greek woman with a deep voice and heavy accent understood. The way her story intersected with mine was orchestrated by God. Dr. Effie accompanied me through my deepest pain and helped me walk to the other side.

Whether harm takes place inside or outside the home, racism crushes the spirit. Some of us may try to feel safe enough by becoming bigger, louder, angrier, or abusive. Others may do so by becoming smaller, compliant, or invisible. The damage of racialized abuse compromises our ability to feel safe enough in the ways that God intends. How can we possibly heal when we are hurt? And how do we move forward knowing it may happen again?

Divine intervention changes everything. God seeks to heal our wounds and fight our battles. There may be incremental change, sudden shifts, or needed patience. Genesis 26:20-23 offers such an allegory:

> But then the shepherds from Gerar came and claimed the spring. "This is our water," they said, and they argued over it with Isaac's herdsmen. So Isaac named the well Esek (which means "argument"). Isaac's men then dug another well, but again there was a dispute over it. So Isaac named it Sitnah (which means "hostility").

These wells are metaphors for the opposition and fear we currently face. This includes the historical hatred, unresolved issues, and ongoing conflicts that result in suspicion and sabotage. Like Isaac, whose wells were blocked by the Philistines, we've encountered racist Philistines. The harm happens systemically and in the context of relationships in home, work, and church. Like Isaac, we may experience obstruction that prevents the flow and sharing of resources. Quarrels and accusations are a regular occurrence. If our efforts are sabotaged or insufficient, we may respond with isolation, resignation, anger, or people-pleasing—or any number of other ways of relating. But these rarely change things.

The Lord's provision of healing includes healthier alternatives to the ways we seek to defend ourselves. On this healing journey, we may find seeds of safety planted along the way sprout and grow fruit. Every day Jesus invites us to lie down, be still, and know that we are loved. Although this may be a challenge, we can choose to say yes and receive help to lie down in green pastures. This implies trust and lessening of our worry and frenetic activity so we may lie down in tranquility and peace, knowing we are safe enough.

A WORD OF ENCOURAGEMENT The Lord is your shepherd, all you need is already provided for. This posture results in a deeper intimacy with Jesus and a greater manifestation of the fruit of the Holy Spirit. More love, joy, peace, patience, kindness, goodness, faithfulness, and self-control become evident in our lives. You still must choose God every day.

REFLECT What does it mean for you to feel that an environment or person is safe enough? Who are the people and where are the places?

PRACTICE Pray as you lie down in a green meadow or walk beside a peaceful stream.

BREATH PRAYER The Lord is here to help—I choose Jesus today.

DAY 24

WHEAT AND WEEDS

"Should we pull out the weeds?" they asked. "No," he replied, "you'll uproot the wheat if you do. Let both grow together until the harvest. Then I will tell the harvesters to sort out the weeds, tie them into bundles, and burn them, and to put the wheat in the barn."

Matthew 13:28-30

The weeds our enemy sows are the many things that try to distract us from God's presence and prevent us from hearing his voice. Sometimes the enemy will sow weeds while we're not looking. Sometimes we plant the weeds ourselves. Past racial incidents may lead to accepting the lies of the enemy. Be careful what you plant. Often, it's hard to distinguish between the wheat and weeds. What seemed like a fertile seed for a fruitful plant was a weed, or vice versa. We can struggle to know whether certain situations that pop up in our lives are beneficial or not. We simply want the pain or situation to go away, so we bypass our pain and try to bargain with God. This won't work. We must stop berating ourselves for hurting. We can also examine whether we are operating in a dysfunctional, controlling, or judgmental manner while seeking acceptance. Regardless, we must be more compassionate, patient, and loving toward ourselves. In my past, I've not done this as I followed fads that promised healing, not fully realizing what I was planting. Everything I tried turned out to be weeds. Up grew shame, fear, anxiety, unbelief. These were the fruit of my attempted self-sufficiency apart from God.

We can ask Jesus to pull up the weeds and heal hurts that have spanned this and past generations. The Lord reminds us to not be distracted by the drama and the attempts to rob our joy and peace. We can ask for the ability to trust in him regardless of what we see, hear, or don't understand. Jesus is at work clearing the weeds, stones, and racism that litter our path and cause chaos and confusion. In listening prayer, we can ask Jesus whether our plan of action will be a help or a hindrance. The Word and the Spirit will encourage, strengthen, and equip us to face each challenge. We are also no longer fatherless or motherless. We are children of God, and as members of the body of Christ, we also have siblings and friends. Through ongoing commitment to fellowship and prayer, we can find help to recognize or claim the seeds of racial healing God offers during difficult times. They are still there, growing. While God will accurately identify the wheat from the weeds, reading the Scriptures daily can help pull up the weeds. Then new life can flow—but remember, we are called to be faithful and fruitful, not just to engage in restless activism.

REFLECT Where do you see weeds in your life or in the lives of those close to you?

PRACTICE Create a list of Bible verses that help you focus on God's presence.

LISTENING PRAYER Lord, today I choose to pause and listen for your still, small voice and the peace of your Holy Spirit. As I extend my hands, show me if I'm trying to pull up weeds all by myself. I invite you and caring others to help and support the weeding. In Jesus' name, amen.

DAY 25

GERMINATION

The earth produces the crops on its own. First a leaf blade pushes through, then the heads of wheat are formed, and finally the grain ripens.

Mark 4:28

Seeds go through the process of germination: A seed is planted in soil and grows. Although the conditions for growth may not be optimal, a shoot breaks through the seed casing and roots grow and draw water and nutrients from the soil. Early in life, we are like a tiny vulnerable shoot. Within and outside of home, many of us experience emotional lack and longing. The effects of emotional longing cut across all racial, ethnic, economic, and social lines. While many factors may lead to emotional longing, one common source is unresolved hurt from family, church, school, community, and society. This may have left us insecure or avoidant in our attachment to those closest to us—and by extension God and others, such as church and work relationships.

We must now heal and learn to deal with difficulties in our relationships in healthy ways, or we may simply repeat the disrupted attachment in other relationships. Emotional lack and longing come from the absence of positive attachment experiences and the presence of negative ones. The negative experiences rob us of some positive ones. It is possible to heal relational attachment issues and break cycles. But we must be willing to get help in the first steps toward recognizing the lack and longing. We can reflect on our past and present lives, families, work, and community—including the pain and the strengths that both are and were there. I began to experience this as I confronted my past, released my wounds to the Lord, and renounced my fears. You can ask the Lord how you can be more like him despite the obstacles you are facing. Because God is beyond time and space—who was and is and is to come—we know he can and he is willing to heal the areas in our lives where we still need a Savior.

Despite what we've been told or despite what we tell ourselves, the deepest desires of our hearts are to know God truly and deeply and to be truly known, loved, and accepted by him and by others. This reminds us that God is centered in and through our life stories. The Lord meets the greatest need of the human heart, the need for love. God's love enables us to grow healthy shoots into the world.

A WORD OF ENCOURAGEMENT In prayer I heard, "I'm creating something great that will transform your life and glorify my name. Open your eyes and see what I'm already doing, laying a foundation although there's rubble. From this I will sanctify and transform every experience of the past. In my hands nothing is wasted; give it all to me and see what wonder I will perform."

REFLECT Is God centered in your past, present, and future story? If not, pray about why and how this can change.

BREATH PRAYER Abba is willing to—heal every part of my life.

DAY 26

SEEDLINGS

The Kingdom of God is like a farmer who scatters seed on the ground. Night and day, while he's asleep or awake, the seed sprouts and grows, but he does not understand how it happens.

MARK 4:26-27

When a plant breaks through the surface of the ground, it is a seedling. It's not fully formed and it's extremely vulnerable. This can also be true for our sense of identity as children of God, members of our ethnic or racial community, or members of the body of Christ. Some of us need to face the familiar ways that our identity is challenged by impostor syndrome: that pervasive feeling that "they" will discover that we really don't belong or know what we're doing when in fact we do. This belief goes to the core of our very being, and we end up believing the lies that try to tell us what and who we are. These lies can limit how open we are to receive from God, who wants to love and bless us lavishly.

Are you becoming weary? Like a seedling, you're growing but you are impeded by the same rocks embedded in the soil. You may want to move on, but the question is, "What is God doing, and what do I need to see and understand?" I now see how often I told myself to just figure it out, fake it 'til you make it. I was rarely honest about what I didn't know or that I needed help. I found it hard to overcome impostor syndrome at my workplace, where I was accused of being an impostor or just a DEI hire. So I plugged along, cutting and pasting as best I could. When I'd had enough, I didn't listen in prayer, I just jumped ship without consulting the

Lord. I was easily sidetracked by folk who sabotaged and derailed my dream. I wasn't clear about the dream, direction, directives, or planning. Along the way I didn't ask God to refine my seedling of a dream.

Yet I found hope amid sorrow while visiting the Legacy Museum in Montgomery, Alabama. There is a wall lined with hundreds of large, sealed jars labeled with the name of a lynching victim. Each jar has soil collected from the confirmed site of the lynching. They hold possible traces of DNA. Amazingly, some jars held tiny seedlings: Without being watered, they sprouted. These seedlings remind me of us. We are more than resilient. Many of us struggle yet have kept the faith, we embrace BIPOC love and joy, and we also lament. Despite everything, the kingdom advances, and we continue to hold faith for a better future for our families, churches, and communities.

REFLECT Are you tired of repeatedly traveling around the same rock? What is God doing, and what do you need to see and understand?

PRACTICE Write out how you have been told or tell yourself that you are an impostor, then write the truth that you are not.

LISTENING PRAYER Lord, I surrender my seedling dreams to you. Please conform my dreams, destiny, thoughts, and actions to align with your will. In Jesus' name, amen.

DAY 27

THE FRUIT OF SURRENDER

We are human, but we don't wage war as humans do. We use God's mighty weapons, not worldly weapons, to knock down the strongholds of human reasoning and to destroy false arguments.

2 Corinthians 10:3-4

During a testimony service at church, one by one, women and men stood and gave all glory and honor to God over what the Lord had done. I listened to stories about marginalization and being pushed aside. I heard how God moved through their lives, restoring employment, healing bodies, and delivering folks from addictions. Yet I wasn't sure how this faith fit into my young life. It wasn't until years later, while dealing with my own struggles, that I surrendered my life to that same God. If you haven't already, I encourage you to make a decision today to follow Jesus. However, like me you will have to surrender and leave behind false beliefs, protections, and images. Like every Christ-follower, you will need to continually have a posture of surrender while Jesus persists in revealing who you truly are.

As we awaken to the labels, attitudes, actions, or trauma that resulted from sins of society or our family of origin, we must face the impact of them. We examine how we've constructed walls around our hearts to try to protect ourselves. We may also make inner vows that we will never trust anyone. This includes Jesus. Eventually we become aware that the walls are strongholds in our lives, places where a particular cause or belief is strongly defended or upheld. Behind the walls were shame, fear of failure, victimization, basic rebellion, control, passivity, or addictions. We must acknowledge and demolish these emotional and spiritual walls or strongholds so each of us can tell our whole story of struggles and breakthroughs.

Sometimes tearing down a stronghold is like the renovation of a house because the walls are flimsy or not up to code. If it's time to renovate, we need a structural engineer to come in and assess what needs shoring up or demolishing to be rebuilt. Like walls that need work, our personhood will need rebuilding—building according to God's specification. The Lord will provide the more that's needed. Trust him to work in his time and his way. God knows what is being built even now as the foundation is being laid. It's countercultural and makes little sense from a worldly perspective because God's perspective is eternal. The Lord will meet our earthly needs, so he builds with us.

The renovation or rebuild will not be done in a sloppy manner. Our strongholds start to come down as we prayerfully choose to be real with people instead of believing we are better or less than others, more healed than others or less. We can come out of agreement with these lies. We also demolish any wall of superiority that guards against feelings of inferiority. All of this new construction can lead to having greater compassion for ourselves and others even after falling short. Thorns will still be forced into our stories, but with intentionality and prayer, we'll listen for why and how. And with help from the Lord and trusted others, we can address them so we can be restored and thrive.

REFLECT What needs to be surrendered or demolished? Ask the Lord—what or who may help you do it?

PRACTICE Symbolizing what you're surrendering or demolishing, use your hands to make a breaking motion, then with palms up listen for what God wants to say.

LISTENING PRAYER Lord, I cannot obey you in my own strength. Help me to turn to you, and recognize that the same power that rose Jesus resides in me. Holy Spirit, please tear down my walls, and rebuild me anew. In the name of Jesus, amen.

DAY 28

DORMANCY: GRIEF AND MOURNING

I tell you the truth, unless a kernel of wheat is planted in the soil and dies, it remains alone. But its death will produce many new kernels—a plentiful harvest of new lives.

John 12:24

In Johannesburg, the Malibongwe Mother and Child Haven women committed their lives to Christ. Evidence of an abundance of fruit abounded as the lives of the families were transformed. We got funding for the women to get entrepreneurial training, and some enrolled in and graduated from college. In 2010, however, due to the global recession, increased overhead, and dwindling donations, Malibongwe residence closed. It was such an enormous loss, for the women, the families, the community, and me. I began to question everything.

Often my grief is over being blindsided by loss—in my family, friendships, work, church, and what's happening in the world. I've learned that processing my grief is cyclical. I won't just get over loss and quickly move on. Grieving is not about forgetting. It's still remembering the love and the loss and slowly becoming open to new life. In some instances, it means forgiving, letting go, and releasing to the Lord who and what was taken from us. "Often, we don't only lose something; we also lose our way. Hard-earned gains and dreams for the future seem irrevocably lost. Development is seriously impaired. Grieving is about finding our way again."

Our communities carry racial trauma that is old and is ongoing with multiple losses. We are grieving while trying to map a way forward. Loss is undeniable; in truth, I prefer to stay in denial, but I know I can't. I too must deal with loss—whether it's at a funeral or when things end.

Scripture says unless a kernel falls to the ground and dies, it will not return and bless many. Jesus is speaking of his death, burial, and resurrection, which resulted in our salvation and the gift of eternal life. Our healing journeys also always involve a shedding, just as a kernel of wheat sheds its outer shell. Sometimes the husks are messages received throughout our lives. Systemic racism, racial trauma, and relational dysfunction try to erase, diminish, or ignore us. This obscures who we really are and what we really feel. The husks also represent illusions that must die for the truth to come forth. This includes the code-switching we do.

Beyond our losses, God is willing and able to remove the husks of racism, trauma, and shame. Second Corinthians 4:7 reminds us that "we now have this light shining in our hearts, but we ourselves are like fragile clay jars containing this great treasure. This makes it clear that our great power is from God, not from ourselves." The challenge for us all is how to keep moving forward despite not understanding, despite not seeing, despite the disappointments, and despite the grief. All the forms of grief need to be acknowledged so we can begin to heal.

Our feelings—or the healing of terror, grief, and anger—don't occur in a linear manner. It's more like moving through a figure eight. While the Lord whispers reminders of the promise to us that it's not over yet, we cycle in and out of grief. At some point we experience an upward turn and can live with loss without it overtaking us, and we increasingly have moments of peace and joy.

REFLECT Consider what outer husks of the wheat need to be shed in your life so new life can emerge. Are you cycling through grief? What help do you need?

PRACTICE Place your hand on your head and heart and ask the Lord to reveal the true source of your loss and what it means to you.

LISTENING PRAYER Lord, my people have endured generations of assault. Show me any generational or current pain I carry that needs to be released. Cleanse my heart, head, and feet. We cry out for mercy and ask Holy Spirit, our Comforter, to comfort us in our grief. In Jesus' name, amen.

DAY 29 

THE FRUIT OF FORGIVENESS

Do not take revenge, my dear friends,
but leave room for God's wrath, for it is written:
"It is mine to avenge; I will repay," says the Lord.

Romans 12:19 (NIV)

The psalmist describes how we are forgiven, healed, redeemed, crowned, and renewed. In turn we can forgive ourselves and others. We are called to forgive our abusers for what was done to us, as well as for the absence of what we believe should have been done. Like Jesus, we may cry out, "Father, forgive them, for they don't know what they are doing" (see Luke 23:34). But sometimes we feel like they *do* know. We may still want to them pay. And that is when we become the judge, jury, and executioner. Hebrews 12:15 states, "Watch out that no poisonous root of bitterness grows up to trouble you, corrupting many." The anger, the pain, and the bitterness we harbor can do extensive damage. It also gives room for the enemy to wreak havoc. The bitter fruit that may begin to manifest in our lives includes envy, malice, frozen feelings, rage, and a lack of joy. While we're stuck in unforgiveness, condemnation surfaces and we become very critical and suspicious. We also may become complacent and complicit. This plays out in predominantly White institutions, organizations, and communities (PWIs) where we can't be or aren't honest about what is happening and what we really feel. We may fear we will lose our jobs or standing in the community if we speak up. And yet it's unlikely that change can happen if we aren't real or speaking the truth.

Holding onto bitterness and unforgiveness takes a spiritual, emotional, physical, and relational toll. Forgiveness releases healing of past wounds, restores us, and makes restoration in the future possible. (The process of forgiveness and reconciliation involves repentance: The perpetrator turns, ceases, and apologizes for the abuse and all the suffering caused. If an abuser is truly repentant, then all abuse will stop.) Some of us may realize that what we accepted as normal in our family, church, or workplace was, in fact, gaslighting, abuse, or racism. We heal as we acknowledge how the abuse has affected us and others. We must renounce our inadequate ways of self-protection and give ourselves time to grieve and be angry. The Lord can handle our raw emotions. In prayer we can ask for clarity about what happened and who's responsible. We also ask for help to release to God any unforgiveness we hold toward the person or persons.

We may also need to let go of unforgiveness toward God—even for situations that we're currently in. We then acknowledge God's rightful place on the throne, guiding and directing our lives.

As King David wrote in Psalm 37:35-37,

> I have seen wicked and ruthless people
> flourishing like a tree in its native soil.
> But when I looked again, they were gone!
> Though I searched for them, I could not find them!
> Look at those who are honest and good,
> for a wonderful future awaits those who love peace.

REFLECT Are there people, including yourself, that you still struggle to forgive? Write down what was done to or by you and how you have judged the person or persons. Bring this to God in prayer.

PRACTICE After praying to forgive and release your offender or yourself to God, you can use water to symbolize how the Lord also cleanses you of any residual effects of the abuse or betrayal. Apply where needed, such as hands or forehead.

LISTENING PRAYER Lord, I forgive and release ________________ for ____.
Vengeance is yours; you will repay. If there is something more you want me to do, I listen now: ________________________.
In Jesus' name, amen.

DAY 30

CULTIVATING JUSTICE AND REPAIR

For I, the Lord, love justice.
I hate robbery and wrongdoing.
I will faithfully reward my people for their suffering
and make an everlasting covenant with them.

Isaiah 61:8

In the temple, Jesus turned the tables of moneychangers who were exploiting the poor for profit. Jesus was furious about the desecration and the oppression. We too look around see how the marginalized are trampled on. We also *are* them, and we want to see justice and repair. Isaiah 61 tells us God hears our cries just like he heard the Israelites. God is just as angry as we are and will show us what our part is to bring about justice.

It has been said, "How do you eat an elephant like injustice? One bite at a time." It will take more than just one person. It takes all of us. We eat an elephant like injustice by many people joining together, praying, and then each person taking a bite. We must pray for wisdom from the Lord about whether doing something to confront or repair the relationship or an organization falls to us or to another person. Remember that our willingness to extend forgiveness is *not* based on the abuser accepting responsibility. To move forward beyond forgiveness to true reconciliation, perpetrators must do as much as humanly possible to repair the damage that they caused. For example, a sin such as slander, racist actions, or abuse needs to be openly rectified by confession and making concrete amends for past and current actions that contradict God's heart. Note that it is often not wise or safe for the one who was maligned or abused to be in close relationship with the perpetrator, especially an unrepentant one.

In John 13, Jesus washes the feet of the disciples just before the Passover feast:

> Simon Peter replied, "not just my feet but my hands and my head as well!"
>
> Jesus answered, "Those who have had a bath need only to wash their feet; their whole body is clean. . . . I have set you an example that you should do as I have done for you. . . . Now that you know these things, you will be blessed if you do them." (John 13:9-10, 15, 17 NIV)

A striking thing to note is how Jesus washed Judas's feet knowing that he would later betray him. As we consider our feet, they have an important function of holding up the body and making it easier to move. Back then, folk wore sandals and traipsed through mud and grime, so their feet always needed washing. Their feet, like our bodies, are literally affected by the residue of the world and so in need of Jesus' cleansing and healing.

Nick and I served folk burdened by their past and weary of years of dysfunction and trauma. These men and women were of various racial and ethnic backgrounds, and from almost every denomination. By the world's standards, these folk had no business being together: the physician sitting next to the waitress, sitting next to an unhoused woman. They came and saw long-standing areas of sin, confusion, and conflict, including issues of abuse and racial trauma. These folks learned it is Jesus who washes, repairs, and brings justice, and later they experienced the Lord working through them to bless the church and the world. Our faith must be rooted in the reality that we have to rely on the work of the Holy Spirit. Intentionally submitting it all to the Lord, we release what we do and don't want to see and do. We then are better able to know when and how to do the following:

> Learn to do good.
> Seek justice.
> Help the oppressed.
> Defend the cause of orphans.
> Fight for the rights of widows. (Isaiah 1:17)

REFLECT Why and how are your feet in need of washing? How might you do this for others?

PRACTICE If you are ready, take the paper where you have written about the injustice committed against or by you. Praise the Lord for his faithfulness and promise that he hears your prayers for justice and answers them. In prayer go to the cross and "nail it there." Jesus will deal with the situation in the manner he sees fit to bring about healing, justice, and repair. You can also pray about whether you are to have a role in this.

BREATH PRAYER All to Jesus—I surrender.

DAY 31

SEEDED: COMMUNITY

She did as Elijah said, and she and Elijah and her family continued to eat for many days. There was always enough flour and olive oil left in the containers, just as the Lord had promised through Elijah.

1 Kings 17:15-16

The word *seeded* refers to having seed of a specific kind or number. The love of God is a seed that transforms us. This love is then translated into how we treat ourselves and the love we show one another—and those who don't know him. These are specific kinds of connections or relationships where deep healing can occur in communities where we feel safe enough, seen, and understood. Research shows that positive experiences and relationships can help reverse the effects of trauma. In the context of these relationships, the hormone oxytocin is released and aids in our healing. God provides such relationships, and they are often a two-way street.

We read in 1 Kings 17 the story about a widow, a foreigner in a very desperate situation. God used Elijah to reveal to this widow his love, mercy, and goodness. When Elijah found the widow, he asked her for bread and water. She responded as one whose hope had run out: "I have nothing but a little flour and oil. I am collecting sticks to make a final meal for myself and my son. And then we will die" (see 1 Kings 17:12). It would not be surprising if she related her situation with just a little bit of bitterness. Trust was probably one thing she did not have in great supply (like her food). After all, those who were supposed to take care of her had failed miserably. Certainly Elijah suspected this but responded based on what God had told him. "Do not worry," he reassured her. "But first, make me a small cake from what you have, then make something for you and your son. For this is what God has said: The jar of flour will not run out and the jug of oil will not run dry until the day the LORD brings back the rain" (see 1 Kings 17:13-14). The widow had a choice to make. We can imagine what was going through her head. "Didn't this brother hear what I just told him? I mean, what part of 'no food' doesn't he understand?" It was probably not the first promise she had heard that turned out to be empty words. But for some reason, she believed this prophet and did what he said. The flour and oil did not run out. She, her son, and Elijah were fed. Their needs were met. Miraculously.

Our own healing is critical and important. But we are meant to go outward with it, otherwise we risk becoming ingrown and stagnant. Like Elijah, we must learn that we shouldn't remain isolated. Our journeys toward healing and deeper community require humility and vulnerability on our part. The authentic relationships that God provides will offer us an opportunity to give and receive grace and challenge. Being in community is the fertile soil for the Lord to do his work of bringing out what needs to be healed in us. To move into deeper relationships and community, our imaginations need to be refired so we know what we are striving for. Many verses of Scripture tell us about community and all the good things associated with it. Romans 12:10-13 (NIV) tells us, "Be devoted to one another in love. Honor one another above yourselves. Never be lacking in zeal, but keep your spiritual fervor, serving the Lord. Be joyful in hope, patient in affliction, faithful in prayer. Share with the Lord's people who are in need. Practice hospitality." These verses give us a sense of some heart attitudes and actions needed to forge community. When you are ready, and with God's directive, you can step into deeper relationship and community once again.

A WORD OF ENCOURAGEMENT You have a friend who is more faithful than a brother. Whether you recognize him or not, Jesus is ever present and ever interceding on your behalf.

REFLECT How has God worked through others in your life—even complete strangers in the most unlikely places—who inspire, encourage, and bless you?

PRACTICE Create a list of opportunities for you to serve and bless others in and outside of your community.

PRAYER Lord, help me to find or discern which significant relationships in my church family, friendships, and family I may lean into, where I can pray and offer ongoing love and support to one another. In Jesus' name, amen.

DAY 32

SEEDS OF VALUE

We ask God to give you complete knowledge of his will and to give you spiritual wisdom and understanding. Then the way you live will always honor and please the Lord, and your lives will produce every kind of good fruit. All the while, you will grow as you learn to know God better and better.

COLOSSIANS 1:9-10

As we look around, we may see signs that we're angry, aggressive, abusive, shaming, betraying, critical, or demeaning. We may exhibit these as a trauma response from abuse. We may believe that only the strongest, the most cutthroat, or the invisible ones survive. Growing up, my story line was "I'm quiet and enjoy moving through life silently." When I was a kid, I didn't acknowledge my needs. I believed that what I thought, felt, heard, or accomplished didn't matter. As I grew older, I just plugged along and sometimes still felt like that child. It took decades to realize that my focus in life was mostly outward. Because it was external, my sense of worth rose and fell depending on what was happening outside. Then the Lord revealed how I sought self-worth and identity from being a helper. What outdated story are you telling about yourself? We may think, *Who'd want to listen or care about what I have to say or what I want or need?*

But we can ask God to unearth these messages and to give us spiritual wisdom and understanding of his will and ways. In the Scriptures, read and listen for how much the Lord delights in us.

God will help clarify our values so they begin to align with how we are to live. We may also choose to share godly wisdom and insights from our own life. As we live in Jesus' power, we can speak clearly and boldly ask Jesus to change our story line to one where we know what we want and need. I've seen this change in myself. Now I know this and can ask for it from my adult self. I also see, by God's grace, how far I've come. I discovered that my underlying aspirational values steered me in the right direction and informed my purpose. Where I was blocked early on shaped what I valued in positive ways, negative ways, or both. The humiliation and racial trauma I faced in primary school resulted in my increased value for justice, equity, and healing. Not always being welcomed created a value to show Christ's love to those deemed outcasts. My father's absence created a value in parental involvement that influenced how I parented. Growing up with lack and in poverty created a value of financial stability and creating much with little. The tragic early loss of friends and family resulted in a value on love and loyalty. Struggling as a teen to express myself creatively through dance, drama, and writing led to comparison and being found wanting. This led to me valuing my creative expression and that of others. Although we may not receive appreciation for what we value or offer, our values and contributions matter. The way we live will honor and please the Lord, and our lives will produce every kind of good fruit. All the while, we grow as we learn to know God better and better. Then we no longer hide our light and what we value under a bushel, we let our light shine bright. In the same way, let your good deeds shine out for all to see, so that everyone will praise your heavenly Father (see Matthew 5:16).

A WORD OF ENCOURAGEMENT Even if right now there seems to be little or low light, you can pray for light and for the true you to be revealed. There is a world waiting to hear how God has worked in and through you.

REFLECT What are you ruminating over that needs to be clarified? You can ask for help in this.

PRACTICE Listen and write the vision. Make it plain.

LISTENING PRAYER Okay, Lord, I surrender my old story line, ________________. Reveal my real story line and uncover my real self that wants to know and to be known, loved, and valued. In Jesus' name, amen.

PART 4

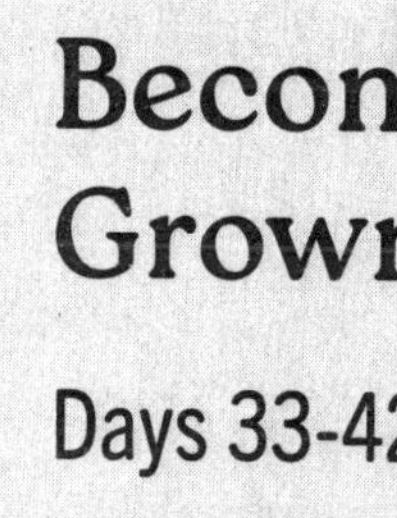

Becoming Grown

Days 33-42

The seed that fell on good soil represents those who truly hear and understand God's word and produce a harvest of thirty, sixty, or even a hundred times as much as had been planted!

MATTHEW 13:23

DAY 33 

THE VINE AND THE FRUIT

I am the vine; you are the branches.
Those who remain in me, and I in them, will produce
much fruit. For apart from me you can do nothing.

John 15:5

We are all on a journey of becoming more like Christ. We are becoming grown. In 1 Corinthians 13:11-13 we read

> When I was a child, I spoke and thought and reasoned as a child. But when I grew up, I put away childish things. Now we see things imperfectly, like puzzling reflections in a mirror, but then we will see everything with perfect clarity. All that I know now is partial and incomplete, but then I will know everything completely, just as God now knows me completely. Three things will last forever—faith, hope, and love—and the greatest of these is love.

This is a challenge to do in the face of racism and recovery from personal and relational turmoil. We can pursue justice as well as love and mercy. We can produce fruit because we remain connected to the Lord. But what happens when, in his great love, the vinedresser calls us to go outside our comfort zone and it upends our life?

As I consider how we show the fruit of God's love, what stood out for me was the interconnectedness between the vine, the branch, and the fruit. As Nick and I struggled with the thought of moving to South Africa, we soon realized how by not moving, we were branches disconnected from the vine still trying to produce fruit. When we finally said yes, it was not because we were convicted or convinced but because we were on a journey. Although the fruit of the Spirit seemed small within and through us, it was growing. In June 2005, we and our two kids boarded a plane as full-time missionaries and tentmakers in South Africa, still working through the racial divisions of the past. After five years, Nick went into complete kidney failure. He still worked as a professor but was on dialysis three times a week. Some of us had experiences that cause us to question God. I certainly have!

The Lord said, "Remain in me, and I will remain in you. For a branch cannot produce fruit if it is severed from the vine, and you cannot be fruitful unless you remain in me" (John 15:4). During that season, we realized that every challenge has a seed of strength that lies dormant or unrecognized. As branches struggling to remain connected to the vine, we could sense God's love still flowing. He was (and is) the source of our deepest love and joy, and the fruit we bore emanated from that love. As the Lord plants new seeds, fertilizes, and waters them, they grow. The same is true for you. The Holy Spirit transforms us from within and eventually we too produce fruit. As we live out our commitment to stay connected to the vine, we see our steps are ordered. Through the vine, blessings flow through us so we can follow the call to love and serve.

A WORD OF ENCOURAGEMENT The Scriptures say, "You didn't choose me. I chose you. I appointed you to go and produce lasting fruit, so that the Father will give you whatever you ask for, using my name. This is my command: Love each other" (John 15:16-17).

REFLECT Are you securely attached to the Vine? If not what needs to change?

PRACTICE Take a photo of a branch connected to a vine or tree branches as a reminder that you are to remain connected.

BREATH PRAYER I am becoming more—and more like Christ.

DAY 34

GROWING PERSEVERANCE

Therefore, since we are surrounded by such
a great cloud of witnesses, let us throw off everything
that hinders and the sin that so easily entangles.
And let us run with perseverance the race
marked out for us, fixing our eyes on Jesus,
the pioneer and perfecter of faith.

HEBREWS 12:1-2 (NIV)

Perseverance involves persistence and tenacity, which are both needed when we keep going to completion in a difficult calling. How we think, behave, and act when faced with a trial, trauma, or temptation affects our ability to grow in perseverance. This is different from resilience. It's been noted that resilience has its limitations: "Imagine that someone has their foot on your neck and it is very difficult to stand up! Resilience is like saying to young people that I'm going to make your neck stronger, rather than focusing on how to get it off my neck in the first place!" Perseverance, in contrast, involves growing stronger as well as the tenacity to keep working to meet a goal even if things get worse. So we work to remove feet from necks—ours and those of other folks—while remembering we work not solely by our own strength. God is helping us to persevere. This combination of persistence and tenacity is a muscle that grows when we bear weight on it. Every time we take a step to meet or overcome a challenge, the Lord enables us to do it. The muscle of perseverance becomes stronger and more flexible, and we're better able to meet subsequent challenges.

Those present at the crucifixion had several opportunities to grow in perseverance. Such is the case with Jesus' mother Mary, who proclaimed, "Do it according to thy will" (see Luke 1:38). Mary Magdalene poured oil from her alabaster jar and was accused of waste. Even when we falter like Peter and face our grief and betrayal, honestly acknowledge our sin, and seek forgiveness, we grow. Perseverance doesn't grow in an orderly way, but with every step we discover meaning and new life emerging from the past joys, pain, and struggle. We find strength from what God has done and is doing now. There is also a great cloud of witnesses in heaven cheering us on as we persevere in faith.

The disciples persevered even as they grieved. They didn't always do it alone; they had each other. The support of churches, support groups, and online or in-person friendships also helps build perseverance. So does seeing a therapist. As we stay present, we discover that we are stronger and not as alone as we thought. Others can hope for us if we lose hope and help us dream again.

We can support our growth in perseverance through holistic soul care practices that prioritize life as well as our emotional, relational, physical, vocational, and spiritual health. As we become more gentle, compassionate, and caring toward ourselves, it becomes easier to identify how to persevere. Some of the most effective soul care activities are listening prayer, attention to our thought life, body movement, gratitude, rest, play, and prayerful activism. As we throw off the stuff that hinders us, our love for God, our families, and our neighbors deepens.

A WORD OF ENCOURAGEMENT The Scriptures say, "Let perseverance finish its work so that you may be mature and complete, not lacking anything" (James 1:4 NIV).

REFLECT Is the muscle of perseverance growing in you? If not, what and who do you need?

BREATH PRAYER Not by might nor power—but by the Holy Spirit.

DAY 35

PRUNING

I am the true grapevine, and my Father is the gardener.
He cuts off every branch of mine that doesn't produce fruit,
and he prunes the branches that do bear fruit
so they will produce even more.

John 15:1-2

For many years I worked hard and yet produced so little fruit. My output was frequently just mixed unripe fruit and aborted attempts at cutting back. In one season of my life, I was weighed down by so many roles and responsibilities that I felt as if I were sinking in quicksand. Yet I continued to add onto an already overloaded schedule. At home, work, and at church I had difficulty saying no or even "please let me think or pray about it first." Over two decades ago, the pruning began as my husband Nick and I felt God's call to abide in him and to love our BIPOC and White neighbors in our proximity and halfway around the world. For Nick and me, the pruning continues even after returning to the US.

Sometimes, we may mistake pruning for God's punishment. But there were things in our life that need pruning. Those areas were overgrown, invasive, or destructive. To get fit for the long haul, we need this cutting back. Pruning is never pleasant; it hurts to cut what we once thought of as so important: the people, places, and things that need to be addressed so we grow and bear more fruit. Sometimes when we look back, we find that what we thought was so important seems like wasted time. I know what it's like to spend too much time crying and clinging when I really needed to let go and let God do whatever he would, to trust that he would give me what I really need—not always what I want, but what will really help me to grow. New growth will require pruning and detachment from what we've outgrown or is distracting or disruptive.

Every autumn I saw this when I pruned our rose bush. Pruning helped keep it healthy in colder weather and, in the summer, it was full of vibrant white blooms with yellow centers. I also needed pruning because I easily became tired of the grind culture, too much pulling on me, and overbooking my schedule. I had to lay down my striving and follow the Holy Spirit. Several times while in prayer, the response I got to my request for more of the power of the Holy Spirit was, "If you do less I will do more." The Lord may call each of us to do less even as we struggle to believe that he will make up the difference.

A WORD OF ENCOURAGEMENT In prayer I heard, "To give you more, you need to let go of what you think you need to have. It's taking up space for things I want to give. Be ruthless; ask me, 'Do I really need this?' Trust me to provide. Focus on me rather than counting the days until 'it is over' or getting lost in obsessing about the future."

REFLECT Is the Lord calling you to do less so he will do more? Be specific.

PRACTICE Experience solitude. Take a slow walk in nature or sit by candlelight and repeat a breath prayer.

LISTENING PRAYER Lord, I trust you; help me to understand that the key is not to just say no to certain things but to say yes to life and life more abundant. Although it's scary, I welcome pruning and refining as hard as it is. As I abide in you, Lord, and surrender to pruning, please release me from the pull and exhaustion of striving. In Jesus' name, amen.

DAY 36

BLOSSOMING PEACE

Fix your thoughts on what is true, and honorable,
and right, and pure, and lovely, and admirable.
Think about things that are excellent and worthy of praise.
Keep putting into practice all you learned and
received from me—everything you heard from me
and saw me doing. Then the God of peace will be with you.

PHILIPPIANS 4:8-9

There are several biblical stories about Jesus and his disciples on a boat. One striking story is in Matthew 8:23-27, where the disciples are in a boat and Jesus is asleep in the stern. The winds and waves violently rock the boat. The disciples are terrified, but Jesus sleeps so peacefully. He doesn't seem to notice or feel the tossing of the boat. How could he not? Perhaps we are like the disciples, and we believe that Jesus is preoccupied and we're on our own. There is no help, so we've got to do something to save ourselves and the others. We look to the hills: Where does our help come from? We doubt it comes from the maker of heaven and earth. So we get our hands on the oars and paddle wildly, trying to make it safely to the shore.

The Philippians verse is not about bypassing our feelings. Our feelings play a vital role in alerting us to something off involving a person, place, or thing. Yet every day we also need peace—not a Pollyanna type that denies the pain, but one that finds hope in the unlikeliest places. When the crosscurrent pull is strong, we need to regularly experience even the tiniest bit of peace or reassurance to stay afloat. On land, we dig our toes into moving sand, trying to stay erect. Off balance, we regain equilibrium, bracing for a fall, but the waves subside. We then feel peace flowing and an unexpected calm. We sense Abba is present. He says, "I give not as the world gives" (see John 14:27). His peace brings calm and safety from all that rages. Jesus calls the waves to calm, "peace be still," and to know that God has not abandoned you. Although Jesus is sleeping in the back of the boat, he is aware of what is happening. One author wrote, "How much of our best participation may not be paddling madly but floating on the currents that take us all home?" Jesus is forever also extending an invitation to turn to him. He has a loving plan to rescue us. Sometimes the wind and waves within us subside as the Lord works through good counseling, medication, and compassion. We find help that addresses our anxious thoughts, brings quiet, and allows peace to become more grounded in us. So, today look for and receive God's care through the Word and through others as all of creation praises his name.

A WORD OF ENCOURAGEMENT Abba says, "Stop trying so hard to prove your worthiness. You're worthy because I say you are. For the blood of Jesus shed for you is all-sufficient. Enough: no more, no less; stop trying, they aren't noticing the extra mile and the cost anyway. It's for me, not them, and I say, 'That's enough, I receive it; well done.' Today I encourage you to relax the grip on the paddle and know that you can peacefully float on the waves of the Holy Spirit."

REFLECT Take a moment to think and pray about three things the Lord is saying to you about peace. Write it down; make it plain.

PRACTICE If you can find a body of water, sit, watch, and listen to the wind and waves and for the voice of God in prayer.

BREATH PRAYER I am worthy of peace—because God says so.

DAY 37

DEEPLY ROOTED REST

In repentance and rest is your salvation,
in quietness and trust is your strength.

Isaiah 30:15 (NIV)

It felt like ages since I slowed down, just rested and revived with no agenda or looming deadline. After a long day of ministry, I returned home to our cat lying curled in a ball on the wood floor, soaking in the warmth of the sun. I longed to enter the slowness. Then I read Jesus' words, "I've come that you will have life more abundant, life to the full" (see John 10:10). But what does that look like, and is it possible to have a full heart that pursues rest that is also deep and strong?

Our greatest enemy comes to us in the many things that distract and prevent us from returning to the Lord. We may struggle to listen because of the noise and chaos in this season. We wonder how we can find rest, which implies the end of wandering. Rest is a safe-enough posture to settle down rather than striving and struggling. In several ways rest is beyond understanding. Rest does not deny the trauma and trial all around. Deep rest contains rootedness and knowledge that underneath, the everlasting arms of love are always carrying us, even if we don't feel it. Rest comes in God's presence.

The Lord offers us rest now and eternally. On the cross, Jesus said, "It is finished" (John 19:30). Under his new covenant, we can find rest from our exhaustion. Rest is a lifestyle, not a moment. This rest is like the water that Jesus offers from a deep, limitless well. We can drink it daily, living in communion with the Father, the Son, and the Holy Spirit and with each other. Rest is found each day in pockets of time as we sit quiet, listen, sleep, and ask. It's time for us to revive old and establish new rhythms of rest. We start by praying and examining how we prioritize our relationship with God, our time, talent, and finances. Do these align with what we say about how we value rest? Each day we must choose to let go of the need to medicate our fears and anxieties with caffeine, busyness, and stuff.

Many of us on the front lines of justice, racial reconciliation, and compassion initiatives and ministries face relentless live and online backlash. However, as we rest, we recover and heal. Then we're better equipped to give, receive, and do justice work that also serves and blesses folk in healthier ways. If we create margin or space in our lives to pause, we experience moments where light, love, and rest rain down despite the circumstances.

While we rest, Jesus cares for the part of us that is tired and weak and feels ill-equipped. He says, "Come to me, all of you who are weary and carry heavy burdens, and I will give you rest" (Matthew 11:28). When his deep rest kicks in, things change. The goals of the flesh and the world lose their shine. Instead, we recognize the Father's goals. These are specific moments that help us to return and rest in God; such as reading the Word, prayer, worship, praise, solitude, listening, dancing, singing, and being in nature. The Lord also offers pockets of rest while enjoying time with family, friends, and even our noisy neighborhoods. In all of these we may find rest where we can just be and it's all good.

A WORD OF ENCOURAGEMENT In prayer I heard, "You can't give what you don't have. You can't offer respite, reflection, or a slower pace if you are not committed to doing it. If you really want it, fight for it and guard it."

REFLECT Are there areas in your life where you need deep rest, and if so, how will you obtain it?

LISTENING PRAYER Lord, as I place my hand on my heart, please remind me of your love and presence once again. It's only from you that we can fully live and move and have our being. Lord, please heal me even on a cellular level. I am exhausted. I welcome your rest. In Jesus' name, amen.

DAY 38

SEEDS OF GRATITUDE

Then your faith will grow strong in the truth you were taught, and you will overflow with thankfulness.

COLOSSIANS 2:7

In the desert, ingratitude and fear were two major issues the Israelites struggled with. Despite how the Lord provided, Egypt still held their hearts captive. They forgot how God delivered them, and they failed to appreciate all that he was doing. We are no different. The Scriptures talk about the importance of memory. All those feasts and celebrations call us to remember not only the good things. They also challenge us to remember the personal or the collective past of our family. As we look at our whole story in America or our home country, we notice there was good, bad, trauma, or seeming indifference. We may also find gratitude and fearlessness in our family line. This helps guard against the pessimism that says nothing good has ever happened or ever will. Gratitude helps remove nihilism because we have seen the hand of God move in our own life. We've experienced things that we can't explain and feelings that surprise, astound, and delight. We wish we could grab hold of these feelings and experience them every day. But every day is not a mountaintop, instead offering little treasures and moments to pay attention to. Some days it's just solitude and silence for us to drink in. Yet even in the noise and some of the harshest realities, God shows up and changes the circumstances and the trajectory of our lives. Even when change doesn't happen, we see how God is loving and omnipotent. Like a sponge soaking in water, we receive the refreshment of the Holy Spirit. The Lord may give us a vision, and we may experience a taste of it. We're excited, then fear and anxiety creep in, and we can feel like we are drowning. Instead of continuing to move forward, we believe the good experience was an anomaly, won't last, or that our dream or calling won't be fulfilled. We begin to act, overact, or under-react out of fear of punishment or failure.

When our child was in primary school, my husband watched the soccer team practice. What he saw troubled him a bit. On the field, our child was hovering on the margins, afraid to commit fully to playing. Later during the ride home, our child confessed fear of looking incompetent with the ball. So the "solution" was lurking on the margins of the action, meekly raising a hand for a pass. In soccer, if you play the game halfheartedly, you end up getting hurt. Even as Nick was explaining this, he felt convicted about how he sometimes held back from what God wanted him to do. As a Black man he was concerned about the reaction of folk. The exhortation was simple: Jump in! Who cares how we look? Get in there; we may suffer a few lumps, but when all is done, there will be great satisfaction because we've been faithful to what we were called to do. Remember, the call for us to walk grateful and fearless may feel difficult if not impossible without a sense that there is One who is Lord over all helping us take one step at a time.

A WORD OF ENCOURAGEMENT Abba says, "Be grateful and believe me and trust in my ways. Dive into the deep end of the pool. I am a skilled teacher and I've trained you. You know how to swim with the seemingly big fish, I go with you, so stop waiting around poolside or wading in the shallow end of the pool."

REFLECT Is there something the Holy Spirit is whispering in your ear? What's holding you back?

BREATH PRAYER His peace guards my heart—and mind in Christ Jesus.

DAY 39

GROWING HUMILITY

For by the grace given me I say to every one of you: Do not think of yourself more highly than you ought, but rather think of yourself with sober judgment, in accordance with the faith God has distributed to each of you.

ROMANS 12:3 (NIV)

Because I didn't want to appear overly proud or conceited, it was hard to sit with or celebrate the ways the Lord has moved through me, but that's not true humility. Humility is a posture and attitude that is free of arrogance or pride. Humility prepares the soil of our hearts to be receptive so the word planted deep within us can thrive. The health of our souls depends on humility and memory. When we remember, we can humbly remind ourselves of what God has done, is doing, and will do in our lives that we can't do for ourselves. Failure to remember invites arrogance, and we forget how we were healed in the past. This can make us prone to relapse into old sin or dysfunctional patterns.

First Kings 17 reveals a deeper issue that God wanted to address with this widow who humbly honors Elijah's request for food. One day her son takes ill and passes. Her reaction is swift, immediate, anguished, and angry—and is directed against the prophet Elijah, the one who represented hope to her. The widow is in deep pain. She was familiar with loss, and now she loses her son. Is this the reward for her risk? On Elijah's side, all he did was obey God and asked for food. However, a holy moment takes place here. This is transference, where one person's unconsciously retained and suppressed feelings and desires of the past are directed toward someone else, who has no idea what's going on. The widow's anguish was about all the hurt and suffering that she endured, for which there was no healing. But the loss of her son was simply too much. Elijah was the target of this woman's searing pain. God allows this for a very specific reason: The pain locked away needed to surface.

This is one of the ways the body of Christ can minister to each other, although it is not always comfortable. Like Elijah, we may deal with somebody, and suddenly, that person is our bossy mother, angry father, abusive boss, or racist salesperson. We react accordingly or completely out of proportion to the event at hand. If we are sensitive to the Spirit's prompting, we can ask, "Where did that come from?" This is where God highlights the need for healing and resolution. The widow needed to know that God really understood her pain, and God exposed it to heal her. She humbly committed her son to the prophet Elijah. The widow's choice resulted in two great things. First, by the power of the Holy Spirit, God moved through Elijah to restore life to her son. Second, God restored life to her heart. Her proclamation makes this clear: "Now I know that you are a man of God and that the word of the Lord from your mouth is the truth" (1 Kings 17:24 NIV). The widow humbly encountered the living God, who is trustworthy, and was then able to trust another. May the same be true for us.

A WORD OF ENCOURAGEMENT For the rest of her life the widow would remember Elijah, and likely humility surfaced as she was acutely aware of how God initiated and sustained her and her son's healing. The same is true for you.

REFLECT How do you struggle with humility?

BREATH PRAYER I humbly give and—I receive the grace of God.

DAY 40

THE FRUIT OF TRUTH

We will not be influenced when people try to trick us with lies so clever they sound like the truth. Instead, we will speak the truth in love, growing in every way more and more like Christ, who is the head of his body, the church.

Ephesians 4:14-15

Life is complex, people are complex. We don't fit into nice, neat boxes. The Scripture tells us to speak the truth in love, but what does that mean in the age of alternative facts and in the age of outrage? How do we tell the truth when it's hard and do so without judgment, shame, or the desire for revenge? This was my experience in counseling sessions. During the first sessions it was a challenge to tell my whole story, but slowly I entered the process while learning to trust my therapist. As I grew deeper in Christ's love instead of silence, I decided to speak up and I reclaimed my voice. You also have been given a unique story to tell, one that nobody else has.

Speaking the truth is a radical and prophetic act. That's why God called his prophets at specific times and places—usually when people forgot who God is or they were believing or living an outright lie, a half-truth, or some mythical story. We can speak the truth in love even when we need to share the most difficult and contradictory emotions and desires. Look at King David and Nathan, the prophet. Nathan loved David and believed there was a calling of God on his life. This enabled Nathan to speak the truth. He told King David a story that exposed the truth that David abused his power when he summoned Bathsheba and was responsible for the death of her husband.

It has been said that truth without love is brutality, and love without truth is hypocrisy. How might God want us to speak prophetically? Nathan needed courage; so do we. We may speak, ignoring the ones out there demanding that we "not talk about that." We will need courage. Yes, count the cost. Ultimately Nathan's words led to David's repentance and spiritual healing. If the Lord compels us, then tell the truth anyway. It may result in our healing or somebody else's. God knows the whole story. And there are times he wants us to tell it. When we tell the truth in love, we may offer a gift that validates elements of another person's story and helps them on the road to healing. Under the wisdom and leading of the Holy Spirit, tell it. Let those who hunger know where bread may be found. Comfort others with what you have received (see 2 Corinthians 1:3-5). We can repeatedly ask the Lord to help us see ourselves and others as he sees us. And remember, the enemy is defeated by the blood of the Lamb and by our testimony (see Revelation 12:11).

A WORD OF ENCOURAGEMENT In prayer I heard, "May the words you speak be a healing balm, a word of hope for those who are desperately seeking me in the middle of the mess of trauma and racism and the way these things combine to warp souls. I am the mighty Lord of Hosts, who saves his people from destruction. Receive my peace and authority. Know my grace, peace, and joy in the Holy Spirit. I am your strength. May you rely on this, rather than your own. Hear these words: *peace and authority.* May you rest in the knowledge that I look after my children, and I am determined to make them whole."

REFLECT When you have spoken up, how can you fully reclaim your voice? Who are some of the people the Lord is calling you to speak and listen to?

PRACTICE Play a worship song and get moving. Praise God with your voice and your body!

BREATH PRAYER I will speak—the truth in love.

DAY 41

BEDROCK

Though the rain comes in torrents and the floodwaters rise
and the winds beat against that house,
it won't collapse because it is built on bedrock.

MATTHEW 7:25

Perhaps we haven't been honored for our part or a role we held; if so, there is something deeply flawed about how we were treated. In all its senses, *honor* means to respect, esteem, or value a person. Although we may not see the full impact of honor, when we seek it for ourselves and others, it may inform how we live, behave, and treat others. When we treat others with honor and live with integrity, what we believe and value matches what we say or do. Integrity and honor are the opposite of hypocrisy.

In Matthew's Gospel, Jesus tells the parable of the wise and foolish builders. The story can be a metaphor that reveals the presence and absence of honor and integrity. Jesus compares the builders. One house was built on a solid rock. And as every builder knows, the quality of our work will always get tested. Jesus says, "the rain came down, the streams rose, and the winds blew and beat against that house" (see Matthew 7:25). And as we expect, the one built on bedrock was able to stand. Another house was built on sand. We see this in the various ideas and proposals of what a good life or society looks like, but there is no commitment to the One whose image we bear. The builder wants the same type of house as the one built on bedrock. But the build is done without an architect, or the quality of materials lacks integrity. This house reminds me of how our communities held protest marches for transformation and justice, but the foundation was not set. Any gains were later retracted by people and institutions that were not fully committed to the rebuild.

When we try to achieve things like honor and integrity in our own way, the house can start to fall apart from the inside. Unless the Lord builds the house, the builders labor in vain. Unless the Lord watches over the city, the guards stand watch in vain (see Psalm 127:1). When our lives are built on Christ, he holds all things together, and he is more than able to cut through bedrock to create a firm foundation for our faith. I'm always astounded when I come across a tiny tree sapling or flower that somehow broke through concrete. At some point, seed was sown on or below the surface. Despite the obstacles, the seed took root even with limited water or rocky soil, and the plant grew. Weathered bedrock is especially adept at trapping moisture and storing water to promote new growth, which pushes its way through a crack in jagged rock on a cliffside or city sidewalk. We, too, want to see personal and communal growth and change. We want to thrive and want things to be fair and just. These are very good things and worthy of pursuit. But personal and communal honor and integrity and justice must be cultivated by and for all of us. This requires a deep commitment to follow the ways of Jesus, who invites us to walk with him on the narrow path. When we receive and give his love and honor, we build on bedrock. There is a line from an old hymn that sums this up, "On Christ the solid rock I stand: all other ground is shifting sand."

A WORD OF ENCOURAGEMENT In prayer I heard, "All that I poured into you it's now time to build—in the way that *you* express me, not as a replica of someone else. In a sense it doesn't matter where you live or work, it's who you are and whether you exercise the gifts I've given. Let's work together to build."

REFLECT What and where and why are you building?

PRACTICE To remind you of how you are overcoming, draw or take a picture of a flower that pushed through concrete or rock.

BREATH PRAYER On Christ the solid—rock I stand.

DAY 42

WAITING FOR THE HARVEST OF BLESSING

So let's not get tired of doing what is good. At just the right time we will reap a harvest of blessing if we don't give up. Therefore, whenever we have the opportunity, we should do good to everyone—especially to those in the family of faith.

GALATIANS 6:9-10

I love the beach sand, the grassy mounds, and the thick patches of vines, weeds, and flowers. Beyond these lies the vast expanse of ocean that stretches out for miles, eventually meeting the horizon. It's high tide and I stand by the water's edge, toes digging deep into the sand as the strength of the tide almost topples me over. I stand, gazing, in awe at the expanse. I think about my life's journey until now. It's funny how the grass, plants, and trees always seem greener on the other side. Then when we get there, we see that it's fake grass or synthetic plants. It looked real, then we take a closer look: It's too perfect. I spent many years waiting and hoping for the next future that I rarely enjoyed the moments.

As the waves crash around me, thoughts about life and work interfered with the need to release and surrender to the wind and waves to be present this moment. By the time I reached my mid-twenties, I'd had enough of failed relationships. I was not spurred on by religious conversion. I simply reached the end of hoping that this newest one was "the one." I promised myself that I would wait, and while doing so, I'd learn to care for myself and my neighbors. We also experience times of waiting in our work against racism. Although our seed is planted, we may struggle, fearing our hopes for ourselves and our people will not be realized. We may begin to lose faith while waiting and feel stuck or tempted to give up right before our harvest comes in. But one day the seed "planted" in us will grow from a tiny shoot to a plant blossoming into the extraordinary. But we'll have to wait.

I think about the woman with the issue of blood whose story is recorded in Mark 5:24-34. A large crowd followed and pressed around Jesus. A woman was there who had been suffering from hemorrhaging and waiting for twelve years to be healed. As the woman touched the hem of Jesus' garment, her bleeding immediately stopped, and she felt in her body that she was free from her suffering. Jesus kept looking around to see who had touched him. Jesus stopped and waited for the woman to show herself and to tell her whole story, her whole truth. Because Jesus calls her out, the crowd sees that a miracle took place. Jesus then proclaims her as a daughter, healed and cleansed. He upholds her dignity and restores her to the community.

Our God is Redeemer, loving and just. Remember that our story continues, so hold onto Jesus. Look for the big and small moments where the light shines in ways that show how all creation declares his glory. Also, we can remain prayerful and open to how our harvest may bless somebody else.

A WORD OF ENCOURAGEMENT Abba says, "The water of the Holy Spirit will cause all things to grow and prosper. Wait and watch. Just as plants take time to burst from the soil, so shall provision and abundance break through. Stop looking to others, look at me.

I, not them, affirm and confirm you. I order your steps. Don't move to the right or left. Follow closely after me because people come and they go, some permanently, some for a season. It's okay to let them."

REFLECT What have you waited for and received, and what are you still waiting for?

BREATH PRAYER I'm brave and courageous—I wait patiently for the Lord.

PART 5

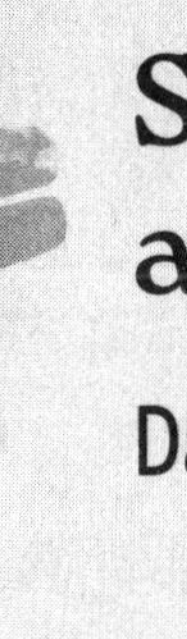

Sow, Tend, and Harvest

Days 43-52

The rain and snow come down from the heavens
and stay on the ground to water the earth.
They cause the grain to grow,
producing seed for the farmer
and bread for the hungry.
It is the same with my word.
I send it out, and it always produces fruit.
It will accomplish all I want it to,
and it will prosper everywhere I send it.

Isaiah 55:10-11

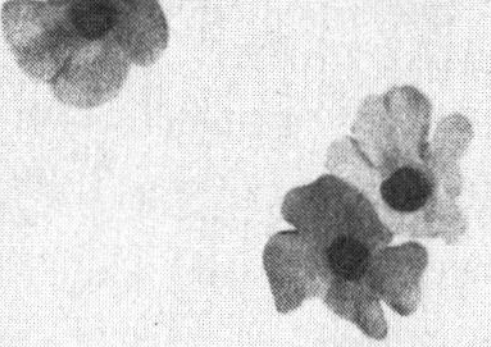

DAY 43

PLANTED FOR GOD'S GLORY

In their righteousness, they will be like great oaks
that the Lord has planted for his own glory.
They will rebuild the ancient ruins,
repairing cities destroyed long ago.
They will revive them,
though they have been deserted for many generations.

Isaiah 61:3-4

This is a fitting final theme. The right condition causes the seeds of righteousness and praise to grow and spread. This happens as we care for others with the care we have received. I've received care and comfort over many years and have accompanied folks during their most trying times. Sometimes I thought I had little to offer. The seeds I planted a long time ago hadn't sprouted. Then in prayer I heard, "Look at what you have. Look around and see provision is coming from everywhere. It is no longer hidden from you. It will be clear if it's temporary, permanent, or eternal in my hands. Ask me to expand your vision to see what is not immediately obvious or what you've dismissed, overlooked, or undervalued. All that you need is here."

After almost eleven years in South Africa, led by the Lord to plant Malibongwe Mother and Child Haven and Rebecca's Well Projects, with Nick's work at St. Augustine College, we got the call to return home. We were overwhelmed at our farewell party and wept as many gave testimony. We were especially moved by one of Elsie's two nieces. The eldest one recounted how Elsie became their mother after their birth mom died. Soon they became homeless and often spent the night sleeping in a nearby park. Then they wandered into the church from the cold. Because God led Elsie's family to the church at just the right time, her life was transformed. The family was the first to move into Malibongwe Transitional Home for Mothers and Children. I wept over the testimony of the fruit of God in so many lives. Jolly, a board member, pointed to the carved elephant letter openers she placed on each table. She said, "For most Africans, the king of the jungle is not the lion; it is the elephant, Ndlovu. Elephants are a keystone species; their role is so significant that their removal causes dramatic shifts in ecosystems. Here in South Africa if your last name is Ndlovu, it's likely you have a royal heritage. Although you were not born in Africa, you're African in every way. God is pleased with you and what you have done. He has renamed you; your surname is now Ndlovu."

Now when I look back, I see how God patiently and faithfully called, carried, and kept us. First Corinthians 3:7-8 reminds me that all of this was and is a group effort. It says,

> It's not important who does the planting, or who does the watering. What's important is that God makes the seed grow. The one who plants and the one who waters work together with the same purpose.

We all need this reminder given the nasty, divisive politics in the United States and around the world, and the turmoil, backlash, racism, and racial trauma we can confront together because we are colaborers with Christ. As such, how might the Lord also want to give us a new name as we bloom where we are planted for his glory?

A WORD OF ENCOURAGEMENT I heard in prayer, "I haven't left you on your own. I want to give you more. Do you receive it without questions or fear of it being taken away? Stop staring only at what is lacking. Look up, and all around, you will see blessings raining down from heaven and on the earth. The fields are ripe for harvest. It's time to harvest the good fruit you've sown over many years."

REFLECT Are you planted for God's glory?

PRACTICE Pray and listen. God may want to give you a new name.

BREATH PRAYER I am colaboring—with Jesus Christ.

DAY 44

MUSTARD SEED FAITH

The apostles said to the Lord, "Show us how to increase our faith." The Lord answered, "If you had faith even as small as a mustard seed, you could say to this mulberry tree, 'May you be uprooted and be planted in the sea,' and it would obey you!"

LUKE 17:5-6

The parable of the mustard seed is a commentary about faith. We may feel we have such little faith, then God surprises us in ways that are totally unexpected. Think about a tree: It starts as a seed, then grows into this mighty plant. In the same way, we can take what little we have, our mustard seed faith, and commit it to the Lord. Then we wait for the seed to germinate, sprout, and grow. So often we don't or can't wait. "This is what the Lord says to Zerubbabel: It is not by force nor by strength, but by my Spirit, says the Lord of Heaven's Armies" (Zechariah 4:6). This is a word for us, too, even though systemic racism says, "Because you're a person of color, having faith is pointless." I certainly experienced this lie in my life at various points, and I had evidence that others had tried and failed. I was told, "Don't bother." Don't bother applying to certain colleges. Don't bother applying for the rental situation, and later, the mortgage.

I'm reminded of how after a night of failed fishing, Jesus told his would-be disciples to go back out and throw their nets out for a catch. Jesus turns everything on its ear. We are imperishable. We can sleep in a storm. After fishing all night, we can even go back out. Although we're exhausted by the onslaught we face within and outside our community, at church, and in our workplace, the Lord says, "Go back out to the other side of the boat." Take a leap of faith; things are going to be different this time. When we consider our limits and frail humanity, we are in the same boat. We also want to lower our net again and be overwhelmed by the catch, knowing that it was God who did it, not us. Today we may feel little hope. But we can take whatever tiny mustard seed faith we have and ask the Lord to take it, and us, and by the Holy Spirit, water and breathe life into our seed to bring forth much fruit.

A WORD OF ENCOURAGEMENT You don't need to always look for the more and the better. It's elusive yet never fully satisfying. In your impatience and scarcity mindset, you don't have to grab it now, believing it won't last. Seek to break the chains of this mindset. God owns the cattle on ten thousand hills, nothing is too big or small in God's hands.

REFLECT What mustard seed faith do you have that may help you to persevere, or is it time to go fishing again?

PRACTICE Look outside for a plant with tiny seeds. Place them on tape and adhere them to your journal as a reminder to keep believing.

BREATH PRAYER Not by force or strength—but by the Spirit of the Lord.

DAY 45

WELL-WATERED GARDEN

The Lord will guide you continually,
giving you water when you are dry
and restoring your strength.
You will be like a well-watered garden,
like an ever-flowing spring.

Isaiah 58:11

I often talk about the resurrection plant that blows around like a tumbleweed. During a dry season, the small gray branches of the plant curl up, forming a ball that covers its seed pods. We may feel this way, rather dry and closed off. But the resurrection plant is one of few plants known for its ability to survive desiccation. It can endure this way for years. It looks like it's dead; however, when it receives water, its leaves quickly turn green and produce tiny white flowers. We may be seeds like the resurrection plant that looks like a weed in desperate need of water and nutrients. It often gathers dust and debris as it is blown by the wind.

I pray for all of us who feel like tumbleweeds. If we could've revived ourselves, we would have. Instead, we can and should ask God to give us water, rest, and revival. In Psalm 56:8 we read how precious our tears are: "You keep track of all my sorrows. You have collected all my tears in your bottle. You have recorded each one in your book." As we openly weep before God, it's as if we are being watered. We are healing and moving forward at our own pace. Once again, the resurrection plant will bloom. We can trust God for water so we may no longer be in drought. We will be like a well-watered garden whose leaves never fail. Restoration includes restoring hope and conferring dignity and honor where this has been denied. As we carry hope for healing and thriving for ourselves, our families, and all of our communities, we'll eventually reap a harvest.

A WORD OF ENCOURAGEMENT In prayer I heard, "When my Spirit waters and fertilizes, you will produce much fruit in every area. There are no shortcuts. After the years of plowing, the seed planting, and small sprouts emerging and growing, you will see the fruit come forth from the labor, even in your relationships—new, good, godly fruit coming forth. Surrender the old way as it rears its head, and accept my new and living way. I am a God of order. First things first. Ask me what's the first thing, then the next, and the next. Don't jump the queue. Wait for me to accomplish my purpose and plan in your life—if you will allow me. Stop with your ideas of what needs to happen and what doesn't. Trust me to accomplish the absolute best for you, for your good and my glory."

REFLECT What do you need to become a well-watered garden?

PRACTICE Pray and extend your hands. Open them to symbolically release to the Lord your plans.

LISTENING PRAYER Lord, I pray for grace and more grace to walk through the things that I am encountering and will encounter. I cry out for hope, love, justice, and the waters of refreshment for me, my family, work, community, this country, and the world. Help me to become an ever-flowing spring. In the name of Jesus, amen.

DAY 46

FLOURISHING

For as the soil makes the sprout come up
and a garden causes seeds to grow,
so the Sovereign Lord *will make righteousness*
and praise spring up before all nations.

Isaiah 61:11

What has the journey been like so far? For me it's been like climbing a mountain in some remote area where the terrain is inconsistent. At times it's flat and plain with little grass, then treacherous cliffs or lush valleys. There have been oases, mirages, wilderness, and frozen tundra. The loss of my mom and the racist backlash I saw and experienced left me in a wilderness. I felt rather lost and alone, wandering in circles looking for something to remind me of which way to turn. I looked for a tree, a bush, or my own footprints. I searched for something to say, "This is the way, walk ye in it." I looked and listened, but all seemed muddled. I felt like our son, who once while in Limpopo, South Africa, went jogging and got lost. He raced around in circles trying to find his way back. Panic set in until he slowed down and took deep breaths. Then he saw the signpost with arrows pointing the way back to the lodge.

Scripture tells us the Holy Spirit helps us in our weakness when we don't know what God wants us to pray for (Romans 8:26). I thought grieving the loss of my mom and the toxic political climate was preventing me from focusing on what God was calling me to. But grief was not an obstacle; it was there to help me to feel.

As I faced what I'd lost, it created space for me to discover what I really was called to. Grief helped me find my way again. You may also need a sense of what you're hoping for, space to move toward it. Without a hope, purpose, or vision, we simply put up with anything. It's easy to get distracted, sidetracked, or give up on our purpose or calling. Proverbs 29:18 describes this: "When people do not accept divine guidance, they run wild. But whoever obeys the law is joyful." The Lord is always working out his purpose in good times and bad. Although we may not understand how or believe it's possible, in Romans 8:28 we learn, "God causes everything to work together for the good of those who love God and are called according to his purpose for them." This includes on earth or in heaven. Our God empowers us to flourish. If we still struggle to believe, "the Holy Spirit prays for us with groanings that cannot be expressed in words. And the Father who knows all hearts knows what the Spirit is saying, for the Spirit pleads for us believers in harmony with God's own will" (Romans 8:26-27).

A WORD OF ENCOURAGEMENT In prayer I heard, "Your calling is uniquely yours, not like anyone else's, because you are who you are. Trust me. You look for the big picture, but what if these are puzzle pieces, and you can't see now how they'll fit together to form the whole vision, something not yet revealed? I'm aligning people and places and resources, don't try to make something happen prematurely. Soon and very soon it will be very clear, your heart will sing, every fiber of your being will rejoice. The people, place, service, and position will feel like coming home to yourself and all that I poured in and through you. You were created for such a time as this, for this purpose."

REFLECT What's the plan? Ask the Lord for the vision and the long- and short-term goals. Write them down and place them where you can see and pray about them.

PRACTICE Open your hands and pray to receive God's plan.

BREATH PRAYER I am called according to—God's purpose and plan.

DAY 47

CULTIVATING GOOD FRUIT

Who is wise and understanding among you? Show by your good life that your works are done with gentleness born of wisdom. . . . But the wisdom from above is first pure, then peaceable, gentle, willing to yield, full of mercy and good fruits, without a trace of partiality or hypocrisy.

James 3:13, 17 (NRSV)

I was moved to tears by Michelle Obama's speech during the 2024 Democratic National Convention. She was honest and transparent about how difficult it was to be back in Chicago, her hometown. The last time she was there she attended a memorial service for her mother. She spoke of her mom in such a moving way that tapped into the heart many of us have toward our mothers. It's not only about who they are or were as women and caregivers. It was about what they taught us. I wept as I listened and thought about my own mother and all the trials she endured and the burden of having to be a strong Black woman. I thought about how she lived her life firmly rooted in her faith in Jesus and the Word. I watched her become the mother of many of my friends and siblings' friends and partners. She treated everyone as image bearers of God and prayed for and with many to find Jesus.

In the early '80s, we owned a vintage clothing store in a largely gay community, and I watched how she engaged with customers. Mom was a staunch, conservative Pentecostal, yet she was always attentive, nonjudgmental, and caring toward every person who walked into the shop. Then a new disease emerged, and many were dying from HIV/AIDS. Richard, a dear Latino friend who accepted Christ, became a member of the church I attended. He was later diagnosed with AIDS. I witnessed how Richard and other men, women, and communities of color faced racism and did not get AIDS education, outreach, or equal access to treatment services. Eventually Richard lost his job, became unhoused, then moved into my two-bedroom apartment. I was overwhelmed by the needs and angry—not at those who suffered but at the people, the systems, and the big-C Church who were ignoring the suffering. Our small church began a visitation program at a local hospital where many men and women rejected by family and friends were languishing in isolation. My mom prayed, but Richard passed away a year after his diagnosis. He was surrounded by a loving community of believers.

Years later I became a Christian and realized that my mom lived by the scriptural imperative to do all things with love. God called me just as he calls each of us to still love. The state of the seed or soil is not the end goal. Sometimes we plant seeds, and nothing comes of it. Then sometimes seed is successfully sown, gets rooted, and grows. The parable of the sower is ultimately about God's word reaching far and wide. Like the sower, we are to mercifully and lovingly sow into folks' lives what may eventually produce good fruit. We do this even if our neighbor is someone we don't know, don't trust, dislike, or don't understand. This may be hard to do, but it's more important than all the offerings, sacrifices, and other "stuff" we do and prioritize in the name of the Lord.

In Matthew 22:37-40,

> Jesus replied, "'You must love the LORD your God with all your heart, all your soul, and all your mind.' This is the first and greatest commandment. A second is equally important: 'Love your neighbor as yourself.' The entire law and all the demands of the prophets are based on these two commandments."

No matter our race, ethnicity, or background, we can be agents of love and mercy.

A WORD OF ENCOURAGEMENT The Scriptures say, "Our bodies have many parts, and God has put each part just where he wants it. How strange a body would be if it had only one part! Yes, there are many parts, but only one body. The eye can never say to the hand, 'I don't need you.' The head can't say to the feet, 'I don't need you'" (1 Corinthians 12:18-21). We are one body. You can be the heart, hands, ears, and feet of Jesus that bring love, mercy, and good fruit to all those around you without partiality or hypocrisy.

REFLECT Has the Lord called you to reach out and love way beyond your comfort zone?

PRACTICE Holding a simple wooden cross may help remind you Christ died and resurrected to free you and everyone from sin and death and to give life more abundant.

BREATH PRAYER My God—is perfect love.

DAY 48

SECURING PLEASANT PLACES

LORD, you have assigned me my portion and my cup.
You have made my lot secure.
The boundary lines have fallen for me in pleasant places;
surely I have a delightful inheritance.

PSALM 16:5-6 (NIV 1984)

Boundary lines can be like invisible doors constructed around our hearts. We can selectively open them and be inviting or close them as we attempt to protect ourselves from harm. When we experience racism or any other violation of our boundary lines, we may develop a variety of ways to feel safe. This includes rebuilding the boundary in our own strength. We then use external cues to create boundaries instead of just stating clearly what we expect. Some of us have few boundary lines. We've endured all manner of debasement and doubt anyone would intervene on our behalf.

There were times when my boundary lines were lax, and I didn't feel God's divine presence or help. I was simply exhausted, and in desperation I cried out to the Lord for more of the Holy Spirit. In prayer, the words *margin* and *boundaries* surfaced. I started small by creating a schedule with margin. That meant having pockets of time to pray, rest, reflect, make art, and dream. I was able to set and communicate clearer boundaries. I could no longer blame folks for crossing a boundary that I'd never set. I also stopped partnering in ministry with folks with poor boundaries—this after being treated badly while investing in their vision even when it wasn't fully aligned with mine. I needed a clearer boundary to communicate how I expected to be treated.

If we do not know how to set a boundary, we can ask the Lord for wisdom about how and where to do it and help to honor it. One way the Lord is doing this is by teaching us how to say no and not be manipulated or used by others. We also can discern when to safely extend ourselves. If we still don't know how, we ask the Lord for wisdom and help to maintain the boundary. Be careful, though: What we often think is setting a boundary can, in fact, be an attempt to build another emotional fence or wall of self-protection. In 2 Samuel 14:24 we read an example of this. After Absalom kills his brother Amnon because Amnon had abused his sister Tamar, King David does nothing. He only says, "Absalom may go to his own house, but he must never come into my presence." So Absalom did what he was told. David sets a boundary with Absalom, but he does so without acknowledging or confronting him about all that happened. There were dire consequences. David didn't deal with the past abuse, nor does Absalom. We later discover that Absalom named his daughter Tamar; one wonders if this was done because of his unresolved pain, anger, and inner conflict about his sister.

We can maintain godly boundaries even if there may be a power dynamic. We may work or live nearby our abuser, but we can ask the Lord to help us to speak up about what happened and if any type of ongoing interaction is acceptable. It's essential that we set boundaries and safeguards and frequently review them. Also be aware of times of vulnerability when we may cross or have our boundary crossed. This can happen when we are hungry, angry, lonely, tired, or sad (H.A.L.T.S.). As we grow, we will make mistakes and will need to redraw boundaries, but we must communicate the change. The Lord doesn't call us to be boundaryless when we need covering and protection. He secures these pleasant places for us to thrive.

A WORD OF ENCOURAGEMENT The Scriptures say, "Then I, myself, will be a protective wall of fire around Jerusalem, says the Lord. And I will be the glory inside the city!" (Zechariah 2:5). You can ask the Lord to be your protective wall, and ask where and how do the boundary lines need to fall in pleasant places.

REFLECT Are there new boundaries that God wants to establish in your life?

PRACTICE If you are you are hungry, angry, lonely, tired, or sad (H.A.L.T.S.), it is time to stop and pray before taking a rash step.

LISTENING PRAYER Lord, your Word says, "The boundary lines have fallen for me in pleasant places" (Psalm 16:6 NIV). Please help me to find spacious places where I feel safe enough and have all that I need. I ask you to help me to continually draw near to you. I also ask for strength to resist the temptations and the pull to allow the boundaries that you set to be crossed. In the name of Jesus, amen.

DAY 49

FIELDS OF ABUNDANCE

Now he who supplies seed to the sower
and bread for food will also supply and increase your store
of seed and will enlarge the harvest of your righteousness.
You will be enriched in every way so that you can be generous
on every occasion, and through us your generosity
will result in thanksgiving to God.

2 Corinthians 9:10-11 (NIV)

As we continue to walk the paths laid out by God, he continues to show his character. One of my favorite miraculous events of Jesus' ministry is the feeding of the multitude in Mark 6:30-44. After a full day of Jesus' preaching, it is getting late, and the disciples suggest Jesus send the people away so they could eat and find accommodation. Instead, Jesus tells them bluntly, "You give them something to eat." This stuns the disciples, who saw the crowd numbering about five thousand. Where were they to get the funds to feed everyone? So Jesus asks them what they have, and the disciples produce a boy's lunch. Not much to work with. But Jesus takes, blesses, breaks, and gives. The twelve disciples take what Jesus gave them, and in faith and obedience they distribute the food. When everyone is full, Scripture says, there are twelve baskets left over. I don't think it is a random coincidence there were twelve baskets. The Lord was making a point. He did not forget the disciples were likely hungry. Jesus was not unsympathetic, nor was he unaware of what the disciples needed. And as if to drive home the point, later in his ministry, Jesus chides them when they obsess over where their next meal is coming from (see Matthew 16:7-12).

This is a timely word. We are aware of the headlines about the vulnerable global economy and the tough times forecasted. We know what the experts say, but many families of color are not unaware of the challenges. Many of us already live frugally or with less while experiencing racial trauma. The feeding of the multitude is a reminder that providing for our needs is no problem for Jesus. Give him what we have, so that he can multiply it. Is the Lord prompting us to share with others from the abundance of our resources? If so, when all is said and done, there will also be plenty left over. Perhaps the Lord is calling us to do what seems totally beyond our resources. Is there "a huge multitude" that Jesus is asking us to metaphorically help feed? Well, what is in our lunchboxes? The Lord will take it, bless it, break it, and give it out.

A WORD OF ENCOURAGEMENT In prayer I heard, "Use what you have in your hands. Give it to me. I will create something beautiful. Trust me to direct and bring order to your steps—the gleaning, gathering, sorting, creating, and sharing that will magnify and glorify me. Leave it up to me, but ask me what it will look like. I am in the midst of your desire to help, just wait and watch. Rest in my love and faithfulness. Do not lean on your own or anyone else's understanding. In all your ways acknowledge me, and I will direct your paths. Again, what is in your hands?"

REFLECT How might you be more generous with the gifts you can share? These may be your presence, time, talent, or money.

PRACTICE Serve in a church or community organization in your neighborhood.

BREATH PRAYER Jesus, I trust in you—you will provide for me.

DAY 50

TENDING WITH PEACE AND JOY

And those who are peacemakers
will plant seeds of peace and reap a harvest
of righteousness [or, of justice].

JAMES 3:18

Throughout my life I've experienced the unseen hand of God offering strange presents. In South Africa, they were gifts wrapped up in strange packaging. Frequently neighborhoods had roving blackouts; the lights went out and it was pitch black for hours on end. It forced me to put down my computer. My feeling of overwhelm was a consequence of not recognizing God holding me and all the things together. I asked the Lord to take his rightful place above all people, things, and situations. There in our house, dimly lit by candles, I accepted the invitation of the Lord to something new, to more peace and joy.

The Word says that "because of the joy awaiting him, [Jesus] endured the cross, disregarding its shame. Now he is seated in the place of honor beside God's throne. Think of all the hostility he endured from sinful people; then you won't become weary and give up" (Hebrews 12:2-3). Keep moving and look for traces of joy. Holy curiosity calls us to remember that mystery is at the heart of the world; it calls us to break out of our tired visions of life. "We are responsible for cultivating beauty in the world wherever we are, to participate in the world's transformation."

So we acknowledge racial trauma and combat racism but we will also celebrate BIPOC love, peace, joy, and wonder. Our people have kept the faith, continue to aspire for a brighter future, and powerfully minister in our churches and communities. Amid tragedy and trauma, we love, work, thrive, and struggle. And the Lord continually saves and brings grace, new life, beauty, and justice. Although we will undoubtedly face racism in the future, remember the Lord and others can help us pray and respond to racist incidents, microaggressions, and racial trauma.

As we continue to share our stories and those of our people, we're planting seeds that proclaim the promises of God. One such promise is found in James 3:18: "Those who are peacemakers will plant seeds of peace and reap a harvest of righteousness [or, of justice]." This is our hope and prayer.

A WORD OF ENCOURAGEMENT In prayer I heard, "Be still and quiet in your soul. I have not abandoned post. I'm at work; surely it will be clear."

REFLECT When was the last time you felt peace and joy? How can you experience more of this?

PRACTICE Create art, cutouts, or a photograph that depicts peace and joy in your life.

PRAYER Lord, thank you for surprise and sometimes annoying interruptions that limit my activities and hem me in. In the silence I remember it is you who holds all things together, including me. In Jesus' name, amen.

DAY 51

WALKING THE FIELDS

For we are both God's workers.
And you are God's field.
You are God's building.

1 Corinthians 3:9

When we grasp how we are beloved children of God and also workers, fields, and buildings, we walk the talk, and we grow. The Lord has told us what is good, and this is what he requires of us—to do what is right, to love mercy, and to walk humbly with our God (see Micah 6:8). Our motivation and vision must center on our triune God and not solely resolving racism, poverty, and injustice—or on our ideas of what is good or right. Rev. Dr. Martin Luther King Jr. said in his last Christmas sermon:

> If you're seeking to develop a just society, they say, the important thing is to get there, and the means are unimportant; any means will do so long as they get you there—they may be violent, they may be untruthful means; they may even be unjust means to a just end. There have been those who have argued this throughout history. But we will never have peace in the world until [people] everywhere recognize that ends are not cut off from means, because the means represent the ideal in the making, and the end in process, and ultimately you can't reach good ends through evil means, because the means represent the seed and the end represents the tree.

When our motivation and vision is rooted in God and what God is birthing in, through, and around us, we can find greater peace and rest. We are better equipped to help "bear one another's burdens and so fulfill the law of Christ" (Galatians 6:2 NKJV). When we advocate for everyone, we declare our trust in God to also take care of what our people need.

We can walk the talk wherever we go. So let's work and walk the fields amid uncertainty and chaos while embodying love—which is an action verb, a sign and reminder of the heavenly vision. Some of us plant while others water, but we work together, including White sisters and brothers with the same purpose. This is the godly love that motivates all of God's children. It carries us forward together and ultimately carries us home.

A WORD OF ENCOURAGEMENT The Lord impressed on me how sometimes as a mercy and out of love for us, the Father shakes things up. This snaps us out of forgetfulness, complacency, or both, and should awaken us to love and good deeds.

REFLECT Are you able to walk the talk? Please explain. And if not, how may that need to change?

PRACTICE Take regular prayer walks in your community. Pray and listen for where justice and repair are needed.

LISTENING PRAYER Lord, continue to show me how to live and love in this earthly body, trusting that you love me and you came to redeem us all and to usher in shalom: nothing missing, nothing broken. In Jesus' name, amen.

FRUIT THAT LASTS

Fruit trees of all kinds will grow along both sides of the river.
The leaves of these trees will never turn brown and fall,
and there will always be fruit on their branches.
There will be a new crop every month, for they are watered
by the river flowing from the Temple.
The fruit will be for food and the leaves for healing.

EZEKIEL 47:12

As this leg of the journey ends, take time to consider how God has met you; revisit and review these pages and your journal if you kept one. All of these may help you to remember all that the Lord has said, done, and promised. In Genesis 26:22, after Issac attempted to open multiple wells, he moved on and dug another well. "This time there was no dispute over it, so Isaac named the place Rehoboth (which means 'open space'), for he said, 'At last the LORD has created enough space for us to prosper in this land.'" Like Isaac, we're no longer wandering exiles, strangers, or outsiders. The Lord is doing something new for and through all of us to thrive, including those wandering about rootless. It is not yet here in its fullness, but in the book of Revelation we read, "After this I saw a vast crowd, too great to count, from every nation and tribe and people and language, standing in front of the throne and before the Lamb. They were clothed in white robes and held palm branches in their hands" (Revelation 7:9). We can look forward to all of us being there, every nation and tribe and people and language.

There will be endless worship and shalom where there is justice, righteousness, nothing missing, nothing broken, for we who follow our Lord and God.

As we continue on this healing journey, we will likely face racism and bias and experience racial trauma. However, we can pray for God to lead us to Rehoboth, again and again. May we have profound faith encounters and witness the Lord standing with and fighting for us all. So let's pray, lament, proclaim, and put into practice the words of Psalm 27:13 for us, our communities and all God's children.

> Yet I am confident I will see the Lord's goodness
> while I am here in the land of the living.

A WORD OF ENCOURAGEMENT The Scriptures say, "There will be a new crop every month, for they are watered by the river flowing from the Temple" (Ezekiel 47:12). In the same way, the love, healing, and fruitfulness of God will flow in and out from you. So those in need may find seeds of racial healing that produce godly and lasting fruit for food and leaves for healing.

REFLECT What do you need to become more like a tree planted by the water source?

PRACTICE If possible, sit by water, in a park, or orchard and engage in listening prayer.

LISTENING PRAYER Lord, as I sojourn through this life with you and others, help me to remember your proclamation in Luke 4:18-19 (NIV). It is your promise for continued hope and healing:

> The Spirit of the Lord is on me,
>   because he has anointed me
>   to proclaim good news to the poor.
> He has sent me to proclaim freedom for the prisoners
>   and recovery of sight to the blind,
> to set the oppressed free,
>   to proclaim the year of the Lord's favor.

Lord, help me to stand on your promise that your word will be fulfilled in and through me and all of your beloved children. In the name of the Father, Son, and Holy Spirit, amen.

ACKNOWLEDGMENTS

I am forever grateful to the Lord and many who freely offer the love and support I need to persevere in my writings. First and foremost is my dear husband, Nicholas Rowe, and our family, Alexia, Jonathan, Oisín, and grandchild Cían. I'm grateful for the shared story of love and strength of my Wise siblings—Kwame, Stephanie, Makeda, Salahaldin, Ernest, Robert, Rynel, Yolanda, and Aisha, and their spouses. And always grateful for Gillian and Tracey, my sisters from my other mother, the late Pamela Rowe.

To my circle of praying sisters: Linda Scott, Sabrina Gray, Val Copeland, Natasha Andrews, Pam Christiansen, Dorothy Greco, Louise Walker, Jolly Mokorosi, Phumzile Mthethwa, Paulea Mooney-McCoy, Gillian Rowe, Gail Musikavanhu, Sherry Golden, Carol Powers, Dr. Monique Gadson, Dr. Kim Alexander, Dr. Natasha Sistrunk Robinson, Dr. Candyce J. Burke, Abimbola Pariola, Dr. Christina Edmondson, and digital marketing and research maven, Margaret Chandia—you are each a blessing and an inspiration to me and so many others.

To my agent Barbara Roose, your wisdom, ongoing advocacy, and encouragement are a gift. Thanks to my associate project editor, Rachel Freire O'Connor, for guiding this book across the finish line. Finally, I'm thankful for these past six years with my editor, Cindy Bunch, and InterVarsity Press for creating space for my voice to be heard.

NOTES

7 *They tried to bury us*: Mexican Proverb and popular Latino/a protest slogan.

7 *So we lament:* Emmanuel Katongole, quoted in Bruce Fields, "When He Died Upon the Tree," *Christianity Today*, August 16, 2017, www.christianitytoday.com/ct/2017/august-web-only/reflections-on-cross-and-lynching-tree.html.

22 *These are days to return*: Beth Moore (@BethMooreLPM), "These are days to return to spiritual disciplines of prayer, Bible study, fasting, gathering, worshipping. No new way. It's the ancient path.," X (formerly Twitter) October 3, 2017, https://x.com/BethMooreLPM/status/915196568290160640.

28 *The movement of the Spirit*: Howard Thurman, *Footprints of a Dream: The Story of the Church for the Fellowship of All Peoples* (Harper & Row, 1959), 7.

57 *Shame can hold us back*: Melody Beattie, *Beyond Co-dependency: And Getting Better All the Time* (Harper & Row/Hazelden, 1989), 88.

81 *Despite everything*: See Sheila Wise Rowe, *Healing Racial Trauma: The Road to Resilience* (InterVarsity Press, 2020).

85 *We don't only lose something*: Glen Schiraldi, *The Post-Traumatic Stress Disorder Sourcebook* (McGraw Hill, 2000), 237.

105 *Resilience is like saying*: Shawn Ginwright, *Hope and Healing in Urban Education: How Urban Activists and Teachers are Reclaiming Matters of the Heart* (Routledge, 2016), 54.

112 *How much of our best*: Marilyn McEntyre, *Word by Word* (Eerdmans, 2016), 114.

124 *Truth without love*: Warren Wiersbe, *The Bible Exposition Commentary*, vol. 1, *New Testament* (1989; repr. Victor Books, 2001), 595.

127 *On Christ the solid rock I stand:* Edward Mote, "My Hope Is Built on Nothing Less," *The Lutheran Hymnal* (Concordia Publishing House, 1941).

153 *We are responsible*: Christine Valters Paintner, *The Artist's Rule: Nurturing Your Creative Soul with Monastic Wisdom* (Sorin, 2011), 28.

155 *If you're seeking*: Rev. Dr. Martin Luther King Jr. Christmas sermon, Ebenezer Baptist Church, Atlanta, Georgia. December 24, 1967 (broadcast by the Canadian Broadcasting Corporation as the fifth and final part of the 1967 Massey Lecture Series).

ALSO BY THE AUTHOR

Healing Leadership Trauma
978-1-5140-1041-9

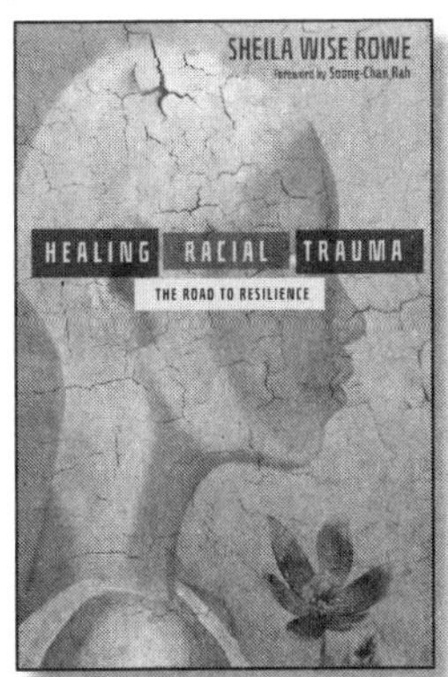

Healing Racial Trauma
978-0-8308-4588-0

Young, Gifted, and Black
978-1-5140-0355-8